World War 2
MILITARY
VEHICLE
MARKINGS

World War 2
MILITARY VEHICLE MARKINGS

Terence Wise

Text illustrations by
John Major

 Patrick Stephens, Cambridge

First published 1981

British Library Cataloguing in Publication Data

Wise, Terence
    World War 2 military vehicle markings.
    1. Vehicles, Military—Markings
    2. World War, 1939-1945—Supplies
    I. Title
    355.8'3   UG615

    ISBN 0 85059 439 1 (casebound)

Photoset in 10 pt Baskerville by Manuset Limited,
Baldock Herts. Printed in Great Britain on antique
wove 80 gsm Vol 18 by St Edmundsbury Press, Bury
St Edmunds, and bound by Weatherby Woolnough,
Wellingborough, for the publishers Patrick Stephens
Limited, Bar Hill, Cambridge, CB3 8EL, England.

Contents

Introduction

At the beginning of history men were decorating themselves and their equipment with various devices by which they might be recognised in battle. Over the succeeding centuries some national devices evolved, but many remained purely personal, identifying a particular warrior on the field of battle. By the mid-12th century AD the system of personal but hereditary insignia, which we know as heraldry, had come into being, and for the next 400 years the insignia used in battle were controlled by kings and heralds.

By circa 1550 heraldry was becoming so ornate as to be useless for identifying persons in battle. At about this date the emphasis shifted from individual warriors to groups of men, from personal heraldry to flags which identified these groups. As the formation known as the regiment (regt) came into being in the 17th century, so men came to be identified in battle by their regimental or company (coy) flags, and identified themselves with the devices carried on those flags.

Flags ceased to be carried in battle at the end of the 19th century. When World War 1 began in 1914, regiments and higher formations in the British Army adopted coloured flashes and badges by which regt or formation might be identified, and these badges were sewn on the men's uniform. As motorised transport became more numerous during the course of the war, so the formation badges were painted on them, to show to which brigade (bde) or division (div) they belonged. The USA copied this system in 1917, and by the time World War 2 began in 1939, most countries involved had a similar system of badges.

For over a decade I tried to persuade publishers that the vehicle markings of both World Wars are the direct descendants of military heraldry and regimental flags, and as such are worthy of at least as much attention as those other two, more popular, subjects: how else are we to identify 20th century military vehicles and their parent units? During this decade a number of magazine articles on the subject have been published by myself and a handful of other enthusiasts, and a few books on vehicle markings have also been published. But neither the articles nor the books have been able to deal with the subject properly, the articles being too short, and the books concentrating on individual countries, and only the major ones at that—Germany, Britain and the USA. Here, for the first time, I have been able to concentrate all the information currently available on the vehicle markings of all protagonists in World War 2, and go into such depth that, for example, the chapter on Germany contains more insignia than have ever been published in one book before—including those books specialising in German markings. For this opportunity I would like to give my sincere thanks to my publisher, Patrick Stephens Ltd, and to their Managing Editor, Bruce Quarrie.

I should also like to take this opportunity to acknowledge the debt I owe to other vehicle markings enthusiasts, and to many men who served in the Allied armies during World War 2; in particular O.C. Costlow, Colonel, Army USAR (Retd); D.D. Delph, ex-4th Marine Div, USMC; Dr Bernard Le Marec; Furio Lorenzetti; Laurie Wright; Mike Jackson, J.M. Andrade, and Les Cable. My thanks also to Colonel Hordern and staff at the RAC Museum, Bovington; the staff of the Photo Library at the IWM, London; W. Milewski, when librarian to the Polish Institute and Sikorski Museum; Lieutenant Colonel Schwulst, Director USMC Museum, and his NCO-in-charge; L.F. Murray, Chief Curator, Canadian War Museum; the staff of State Maggiore dell'-Esercito in Rome; and the New Zealand Army General Staff. I should also like to pay particular tribute to the pioneering work done on Japanese and USSR vehicle markings by Steve Zaloga.

Finally, I would like to acknowledge here the great debt I owe to John Major, a fellow member of the Military Heraldry Society, who, at short notice, undertook the mammoth task of producing such excellent artwork from my working sketches.

Abbreviations

In the interests of space, it has been necessary to use a number of abbreviations, most of which are quite common in military writings. To prevent any possible confusion, the abbreviations and their meanings are set out below.

A/A	Anti-aircraft
AASC	Australian Army Service Corps
AEME	Australian Electrical and Mechanical Engineers
AFV	Armoured Fighting Vehicle
AGRA	Army Group Royal Artillery
AQMS	Artificer Quartermaster Sergeant
Arty	Artillery
ARV	Armoured Recovery Vehicle
A/T	Anti-tank
Bde	Brigade
Bn	Battalion
Btty	Battery
Cav	Cavalry
Cmdr	Commander
CMP	Corps of Military Police
CO	Commanding Officer
Col	Column
Coy	Company
CRA	Commander Royal Artillery
CRE	Commander Royal Engineers
CSM	Company Sergeant Major
Div	Division
Drgns	Dragoons
FA	Field Artillery
Gren	Grenadier
Grp	Group
HMG	Heavy machine-gun
Indep	Independent
Inf	Infantry
LAA	Light Anti-aircraft
L of C	Lines of Communication
MMG	Medium machine-gun
MT	Motor Transport
NZASC	New Zealand Army Service Corps
OKW	Oberkommando der Wehrmacht, German Army High Command
OP	Observation post
Pz	Panzer, armour or tank
PzKpfw	Panzerkampfwagen, tank
QM	Quartermaster
RAC	Royal Armoured Corps
RAMC	Royal Army Medical Corps
RAOC	Royal Army Ordnance Corps
RAPC	Royal Army Pay Corps
RASC	Royal Army Service Corps
Recce	Reconnaissance
Regt	Regiment
REME	Royal Electrical and Mechanical Engineers
RCA	Royal Canadian Artillery
RTR	Royal Tank Regiment
SHQ	Squadron headquarters
SL	Searchlight
SP	Self-propelled
Sqdn	Squadron
TA	Territorial Army
Trpt	Transport
2I/C	Second in command

The Allied Powers

Great Britain

1 National Identification marks

The official instructions for vehicle markings do not mention any form of national identification marking prior to the introduction of the Allied white star in 1943, but several such markings were in common use before that date. The first was a simple white patch between 12 and 15 in square (30 and 37.6 cm), painted on the hull fronts of AFVs sent to France with the BEF. Carriers had the patch on their sides, and soft-skins seem to have carried it on the front left mudguard, although this cannot be confirmed since this particular surface is usually reflecting light in the photographs studied and the patches are therefore not clear.

For a brief period after Dunkirk some of the few tanks in Britain carried a broad white band painted round the lower edge of the turret, but this may have been a local mark, indicating formation or training role rather than nationality. However, by the late autumn of 1941 a true national identification mark had at last been introduced. During the last year of World War 1 it had been found necessary to paint a white/red/white patch on tanks to distinguish them from those captured British tanks being used by the Germans. By November 1941 this emblem had been re-introduced on AFVs in the Western Desert, where the problem had recurred following the arrival of the Deutsches Afrika Korps. The patch was 18 in (45 cm) square with each vertical stripe 6 in (15.2 cm) wide. Location varied considerably, from a single patch on the turret rear to as many as six such patches on turret rear and sides, hull front and sides near the front (over the idler wheels). Sometimes the patches appeared on both front sandshields instead of centrally on the glacis.

Armoured cars and the Light tanks usually carried a single patch on the hull front, some-times repeated on turret rear.

In March 1942 a similar but rectangular patch was introduced for AFVs in the UK, again formed of three stripes each 6 in (15.2 cm) wide, but the height of the patch was now only 10 in (25.4 cm). However, for some unknown reason, the colours were reversed, being red/white/red, and the patch became known as the RAC flash. This was in common use on AFVs in the UK right through until 1944, and with the shipping of units abroad it also began to appear elsewhere. For example, many of the tanks in the Western Desert during 1941-2 had red/white/red patches instead of white/red/white ones. It would seem that most of the Infantry tanks, the Matildas and Valentines, carried the RAC flash, while the Cruisers and Crusaders carried the white/red/white patch, but whether this was a deliberate distinction or not is unknown to this writer. It should be remembered that this is only a generalisation: some Infantry tanks had the white/red/white patch, while many tanks did not carry any form of identification mark. The Lee/Grants in British service in North Africa carried the RAC flash.

When the 1st Army landed in Tunisia its AFVs bore the RAC flash, and in 1943 all AFVs in the Italian campaign also bore this device as a national identification mark. It was commonly painted as a rectangle on both sides of the hull, and often centrally on the lower front of the hull. The flash continued to be used on many AFVs in Italy until the end of 1944, despite the introduction of the Allied white star in the summer of 1943.

For full details of the size and location of the Allied white star on vehicles see USA section 1. However, British AFVs in north-west Europe rarely carried the star, the majority having no national identification mark at all. Softskins normally carried the stars only on their sides. In Burma and the Far East the American system was followed more closely, though AFVs usually had stars on just the hull or turret sides.

The Union Flag has also been seen on vehicles at the end of the war, for example on the turret rear of armoured cars in Damascus in May 1945, but this would appear to be an extremely rare occurrence. Flags were also used to identify friendly vehicles, see section 3 below.

2   Aerial recognition symbols

There were no instructions on aerial recognition symbols in the contemporary vehicle markings pamphlets and no such signs were employed at the beginning of the war. In 1941 two different types of signs appeared occasionally on the upper surfaces of AFVs, and these seem to have been the first attempts at finding a suitable system of aerial recognition. The first type was a 2 in wide (5.1 cm) white border, painted round the outer edge of the turret top, in early 1941. In September of the same year a yellow triangle of fabric was used on the top surfaces of AFVs with radio. Both systems appear to have been limited to the UK.

The need for an aerial recognition system during the fighting in the Western Desert led to the introduction there in 1941-2 of a white St Andrew's cross, sometimes outlined with black. This was painted on the tilt and bonnet top (if open cab) or tilt and cab top (if closed cab with hard top) of softskins. If does not seem to have been used on AFVs. However, prior to this, white/red/white stripes had been painted round the edges of turret tops of AFVs in the 7th RTR of 7th Armoured Div for Operation Battleaxe (June 1941).

The white St Andrew's cross was not used for long, and in January 1942 at the latest in the UK, and soon after in the Middle East, an RAF-type roundel was introduced as an aerial recognition symbol, the outer ring being blue, the inner red, with white between them. Sometimes a yellow edging was added. The roundel was painted on cab or bonnet tops and on the engine decks or turret tops of AFVs. On cabs and bonnets it had a radius of 31 in (27.9 cm) made up as follows: outer ring of yellow 6 in (15.2 cm); blue 10 in (25.4 cm); white 10 in (25.4 cm); red centre 5 in (12.7 cm). The roundel continued to be used in Italy, until gradually replaced by the Allied white star and circle from mid-1943.

Towards the end of the war in Europe, probably from the D-Day landings onwards, AFV crews used panels of coloured plastic on the upper surfaces of their vehicles to identify them to friendly aircraft. The colour for the panels was changed daily in a haphazard sequence: pink and yellow were two of the three colours employed. This system enabled the sign to be instantly removed if an enemy aircraft approached, and prevented copying by the enemy to protect his own AFVs.

From mid-1943 onwards softskins and AFVs in all theatres began to use the Allied white star as an aerial recognition symbol. For exact sizes and locations see USA, section 1.

3   Rank, signal and other flags

In 1930 a system of flags to identify unit cmdrs' vehicles had been established, and this was still in use when war broke out. These flags were used extensively on AFVs in the Western Desert, flown from wireless aerials. Their use was discontinued about the end of 1942. The flags are illustrated in **Plate I Figs 1-4: Fig 1** Bde cmdr, 12 by 36 in (30 by 90 cm), in colour chosen for the formation, and without any markings; **Fig 2** Regt or bn cmdr, 18 by 36 in (45 by 90 cm), in colours of the regt (three horizontal stripes of brown over green over red were used for the RTR) with unit serial number imposed in white, or black if necessary or more appropriate; **Fig 3** Sqdn or coy cmdr, 9 by 18 in (22.5 by 45 cm), red for A Sqdn, yellow for B, blue for C, with sqdn or coy letter or number in white; **Fig 4** Troop or section cmdr, 9 by 13 in (22.5 by 32.5 cm), black with two coloured stripes, red for 1st Troop, yellow for 2nd, blue for 3rd, green for 4th, white for 5th.

One known variation within this system occurred in the 1st Lothian Regt (48th Div, later 51st Div), serving in the BEF in 1940. In this regiment the sqdn pennants were: HQ red, A Sqdn yellow (with sqdn letter in black instead of the usual white), B Sqdn blue, C Sqdn green.

In addition there appears to have been some system of flag code used in the Western Desert to identify friendly vehicles from a distance, one example being the flying of two yellow pennants at the tops of the aerials of all the tanks within a unit. These pennants presumably had their number and colour changed daily.

From February 1941 a Cambridge-blue flag measuring 12 by 24 in (30 by 60 cm) was carried and displayed by hand when necessary. This flag was replaced by the RAC flash, which was introduced about March 1942. **Table 1** lists

Table 1: 1st Armoured Div pennants, Middle East, 1941.

Red   Queen's Bays, 2nd Armoured Bde
Royal Glos Hussars 22nd Armoured Bde
1st Field Sqdn, RE

Yellow 9th Lancers, 2nd Armoured Bde
3rd County of London Yeomanry,
22nd Armoured Bde
7th Field Sqdn RE

Blue   10th Hussars, 2nd Armoured Bde
4th County of London Yeomanry,
22nd Armoured Bde

Green 1st Rifle Bde, 2nd Armoured Bde
2nd KRRC, 22nd Armoured Bde

White 12th Lancers

'HQ' was carried on the pennants of Sqdn HQ vehicles.

---

pennants used within 1st Armoured Div in the Western Desert in late 1941.

Four other flags were employed in the Western Desert during the 1941-2 period. Three of these were signal flags (**Plate I Figs 5-7**) whose meanings and colours were: **Fig 5** red over white over blue—Rally; **Fig 6** green/white—Come on; **Fig 7** red/yellow—Out of Action. The fourth was a blue pennant with a red disc (**Plate I Fig 8**) carried by vehicles of the RAOC, which performed all recovery and repair until 1942 when the REME was formed and by which date the use of pennants had been discontinued.

The January 1941 Vehicle Marking pamphlet carries instructions for the marking of command and staff vehicles: the instructions are reproduced in full below. They were repeated verbatim in the 1942 and 1943 instructions, with but one addition; see item *i* below.

'Command and staff signs will be fitted locally to vehicles allotted to the following:

i) Infantry Div: div cmdr; CRA; bde cmdrs; CRE; GS01; cmdrs of RA regts, div Signals, recce unit, machine-gun bn, Infantry bns, div RASC.

ii) Armoured Div: div cmdr; bde and group cmdrs; CRE; GS01; cmdrs of armoured regts, RA regts, Infantry regts, armoured car regts, div RASC.

iii) Army Tank Bdes: bde cmdr, bn cmdrs.

iv) AA Divisions (added in 1943): div cmdr, bde cmdrs, GS01, cmdrs of AA and SL regts.

'The sign may be improvised from a one-gallon oil tin or similar container, the approximate dimensions being 10 in (25.4 cm) by 6 in (15.2 cm) by 4½ in (11.4 cm). It will be fitted to the rear off-side of the body by means of a bracket 6 in (15.2 cm) above the level of the rear wing. It will be illuminated internally by means of an independent switch on the dashboard of the vehicle and will be arranged to show both front and rear. By means of a talc window the div sign is shown above, and the formation flag and/or serial number or lettering indicating the occupant of the vehicle, is shown below.'

Three examples were given and these are reproduced in **Plate X: Fig 22** GS01; **Fig 23** Bde cmdr; **Fig 24** cmdr RA.

In 1944 the practice of carrying star plates on the vehicles of high ranking officers was copied from the US Army. The plates were red and were normally carried on the front and rear of the vehicle. Yellow stars denoted the rank of the officer: one for Brigadier, two for Major General, three for Lieutenant General, four for General and five for Field Marshal. Cars used by Commanders-in-Chief in each theatre frequently bore the Union Flag, either a small fabric version flown from a metal rod at front and centre of the bonnet, or a metal plate attached to the vehicle front.

Plate I (above right): British rank and signal flags.

Note: Black is shown as such in all plates. If a colour is not given for white parts of the drawings, then those parts were white.

4   Formation signs

These signs had first been introduced during World War 1 as a means of identifying the formations to which vehicles belonged by a usually heraldic badge painted on the vehicle's front and rear. The signs were re-introduced in October 1939 but were only used on vehicles in the UK and BEF at this date: not until 1941 did vehicles in other theatres begin to carry the signs The official instructions issued in 1943 are detailed and well worth quoting in full: those issued before and after this date had only minor amendments.

'The formation sign will be stencilled on the near side front mudguard on all types of vehicles which have mudguards, except motorcycles. On vehicles without mudguards, the formation sign will be stencilled in a position corresponding as nearly as possible to the near side front mudguard. In addition, formation signs will be stencilled in a prominent position on the rear of the vehicle. Formation signs will not be carried on motor cycles.

Plate I: British rank and signal flags.

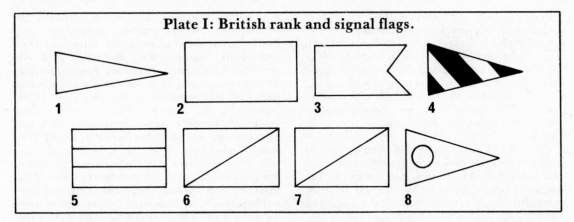

'Formation signs will be carried as shown below:

i) Div sign: By all units permanently allotted to a div.

ii) Corps sign: By all units permanently allotted as corps troops.

iii) Command, Corps district, district and area sign: It is left to commands to decide which units shall carry command signs and which corps district, district or area signs. As a general guide those units allotted to corps district, district or area operational control should carry their corps district, district or area sign respectively.

iv) General Headquarters sign: By GHQ troops on instructions from GHQ.

v) War Office sign: When specially authorised by the War Office only.' (A later paragraph stipulates that this will include vehicles of units, schools, establishments, etc, 'under the direct control of the War Office').

'The following are exceptions to the above:

i) Certain independent Infantry bdes and bns have been allotted special signs. Should such a bde or bn be permanently absorbed into a div, the special sign will be removed and the div sign adopted.

ii) Motor coach coys, reserve MT coys and troop carrying coys will carry command signs, and not the sign of the corps or div to which they are attached, except those allotted to corps directly under GHQ, when the corps sign will be carried.

iii) Coast arty units have been allotted a special sign.'

Needless to say, these instructions were not always followed to the letter. In some units, motor cycles carried the formation sign on each side of the petrol tank. On occasions, signs were hand painted, and rather crudely at that: a man

who served in 7th Armoured Div refers to some paintings of the jerboa, done in a hurry in the front line, as looking, 'more like begging bears with triangle heads and were the source of much laughter'. Stencils were sometimes reversed in error, so, for example, you could have the signs of 1st, 7th and 11th Armoured Divs looking to either left or right. Colours could also be changed: the rhino of 1st Armoured Div appeared as black on a white background in France in 1940, but on the lighter vehicle paint-work used in North Africa this was changed to white on black.

From 1943 onwards in North Africa, and sub-sequently in Italy, many units combined the formation sign and arm of service flash (see section 6 below) to create a single sign, carried centrally or on one mudguard (or equivalent position), which showed all the necessary information concisely and conveniently. Some formations also carried two formation signs: for example, many RASC companies carried a div or corps sign *and* a coy sign, while tanks in 21st Army Tank Bde in North Africa bore both their own sign and that of the 4th Inf Div which they were supporting. In Italy the same bde again carried two signs, its own and that of 1st Canadian Div, which it supported. Similarly, the vehicles of 22nd Armoured Bde carried their own sign and that of their parent formation, 7th Armoured Div, and some independent bdes used the sign of the corps to which they were attached in addition to their own sign.

The January 1941 vehicle marking regulations contain one other interesting variant, not listed in subsequent pamphlets: 'Formation signs printed on paper 5 inches square (12.7 cm) may also be fixed to the left hand bottom corner of the windscreens of all vehicles fitted with wind-screens'.

Finally. many of these signs, and other markings on vehicles, were painted out when in the forward areas, and indeed official instructions were issued in the UK to the effect that formations embarking for overseas should paint over all vehicle markings before leaving their mobilisation centres. The only exception to this was 21st Army Group, which went straight into battle from its concentration areas in England.

There is still some confusion over the actual design of some formation signs, and which signs were carried by which unit, particularly in the armoured bdes. The most recent and relevant pamphlets available when conducting my research, the 1944 vehicle markings regulations, are incomplete when it comes to formation signs, but do give some variations to the commonly accepted designs and colours. I have illustrated those signs normally attributed to the various units, but included in the captions detail of any variants and discrepancies. Correspondence with men who served in some of the units has also enabled me to clear up some old and knotty problems, particularly with regard to 21st and 25th Armoured Bdes, and the various signs employing the jerboa and fox's mask.

The signs themselves are so numerous that it would have been impossible to illustrate them all. Therefore, I have omitted those of the higher formations, which are quite commonly known and in any case were less common on combat vehicles, and concentrated on the signs of divs and lower formations. This has enabled me to include a considerable number of signs, particularly (in section 5) those of the RASC companies which supplied and supported the front line troops, which have not been published since the official pamphlets issued by the Army for limited circulation during the war years. Readers wishing to obtain information on formation signs for corps and higher formations are referred to Lieutenant Colonel H.N. Cole's excellent book, listed under Sources.

Plate II (opposite): British formation signs; armoured formations.

1 Guards Armoured Div: blue shield edged red. **2** 1st Armoured Div: used until just before El Alamein. Also appeared as black on or outlined in white in France during 1939-40. **3** 1st Armoured Div: 1942-4. **4** 2nd Armoured Div: red square. **5** 6th Armoured Div. **6** 7th Armoured Div: red square and jerboa. Used 1940-early 1944 (Africa and Italy). The earlier Mobile Div, Egypt 1938-9, used a white disc on a red square.

The jerboa sometimes appeared on just a white field and was crudely painted by hand, causing many variations of form. **7** 7th Armoured Div: red jerboa, north-west Europe 1944-5. **8** 8th Armoured Div: green disc. **9** 9th Armoured Div. **10** 10th Armoured Div: red. This was predominant in later years of the war. **11** 10th Armoured Div: red on yellow, variant used frequently in earlier years. A yellow fox's mask on a red disc was also used during 1943. **12** 11th Armoured Div: red horns, hooves, eyes and nostrils, yellow rectangle. On tanks in action it was not uncommon for the sign to be represented by just the yellow rectangle. **13** 42nd Armoured Div: red border. (42nd Armoured Engineer Regt used the same sign before becoming 42nd Armoured Div.) **14** 79th Armoured Div: red horn tips and nostrils, yellow field. 1944 regs state white background. **15** 1st Armoured Bde Grp: red tiger's head. (2nd Armoured Bde of 1944-5 used the early standing rhino of 1st Armoured Div. 1st Tank Bde used a red diabolo- inverted triangle joined to apex of a second, see **Fig 23**.) **16** 3rd Armoured Bde Grp: red tank and flash on brown hill against grey (?) background, all edged red. **17** 4th Armoured Bde: 1944 regs give black jerboa on white circle on red square. **18** 6th Guards Tank Bde: blue/red/blue bend on shield and yellow sword overall. **19** 7th Armoured Bde: light green jerboa, red inner border on disc. 1944 regs give dark green jerboa on light green field. **20** 8th Armoured Bde: red fox's head and border on yellow field. **21** 9th Armoured Bde: green field. **22** 20th Armoured Bde. **23** 21st Tank Bde: originally dark blue diabolo. During the Italian campaign the bde was allowed to add the red devil. The sign normally appeared on a yellow disc. **24** 21st Tank Bde: yellow maple leaf on red. Carried on tanks of the bde in addition to their own sign as a unique honour whilst serving in Italy. **25** 22nd Armoured Bde: red stag's head. **26** 23rd Armoured Bde. (23rd Tank Bde used a green diabolo. 24th Tank Bde used a blue one.) **27** 25th Armoured Engineer Bde: red shield, two blue bars. 1944 regs call this unit B Assault Bde CMF. **28** 27th Armoured Bde: yellow sea horse edged white, light blue shield. 31st Indep Armoured Bde, (also given as 31st Tank Bde), used a pale green diabolo. **29** 32nd Tank Bde: green centre, stalk and leaf to daisy. Unconfirmed; the bde did not have an official sign before capture in Tobruk in 1942. 33rd Armoured Bde (also given as 33rd Tank Bde), used a green over black diabolo. **30** 34th Armoured Bde: red shield, yellow bend. This sign sometimes appeared on a black rectangle.

Plate II: British formation signs; armoured formations.

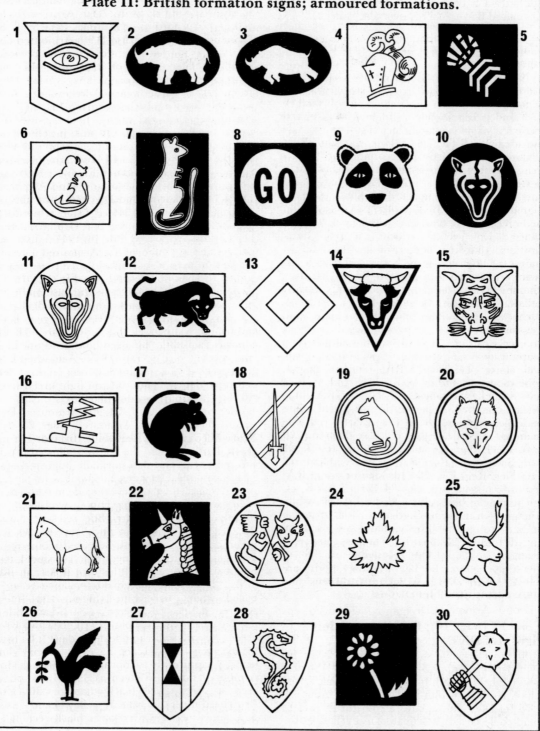

35th Armoured Bde (also given as 35th Tank Bde), used a brown over green diabolo. 36th Armoured Bde used a red over black one.

Plate III (opposite): British formation signs.

1 No 1 Armoured Replacement Grp CMF: yellow over red field. **2** Recce Corps: green field edged yellow, yellow diamond. Unconfirmed. **3** 17th Indep Desert Bde: light blue square, red triangle, yellow arrow. Unconfirmed: the bde included **4** RTR. **4** GHQ Liaison Regt (Phantom). **5** LRDG: red scorpion. **6** Popski's Private Army: colour unknown, probably black, or white on black square. **7** 1st Div Signals: lower part and edging of upper dark blue. Used by Signals units of 1st Inf Div. **8** 571st Construction Sqdn RE: blue 10 on red. Unconfirmed. **9** Royal Marine Div: yellow trident on red. Later worn by 116th RM Indep Inf Bde. **10** 117th RM Indep Inf Bde: yellow anchor and star with red centre. **11** Amphibian Support Regt RM: dark blue shield, inverted red triangle bearing narrow yellow border and anchor. **12** 1st and 6th Airborne Divs: pale blue Bellerophon and Pegasus on dark maroon. Used without difference by both divs. **13** 1st Air Landing Bde: maroon square, red rose, green shamrock, thistle and stalks. **14** 3rd AGRA: blue/red shield, yellow cannon. **15** 6th AGRA. **16** 92nd AGRA: red over blue rectangle. **17** 95th AGRA: blue shield, red shell, upper section of shield white with blue aircraft. **18** 1st Corps Arty: red/blue diamond. **19** 1st Div RA: red/blue diamond. **20** 33rd Field Regt RA: blue diamond, red 3. **21** 37th Searchlight Regt RA: yellow emblem. **22** 74th Field Regt RA. **23** 74th Medium Regt RA: red broken spur on khaki. **24** 124th LAA Regt: red rectangle, blue saltire. **25** 1st Inf Div: white triangle with red or black edges, or white triangle on black square, all three variants were used. **26** 2nd Inf Div. **27** 3rd Inf Div: red inverted triangle. **28** 4th Inf Div: originally just the 4th quadrant of a circle but later as shown: both were red. **29** 5th Inf Div: khaki square. 1944 regs state black square. **30** 6th Inf Div: red star.

Plate IV (page 16): British formation signs; Inf Divs.

1 8th Inf Div: blue shield, red cross. **2** 9th Inf Div: dark blue disc. **3** 12th Inf Div. **4** 13th Inf Div: red field. **5** 15th Inf Div: yellow circle edged white, red lion. **6** 18th Inf Div: orange square. **7** 23rd Inf Div: blue square. **8** 36th Inf Div: right hand circle is red. **9** 38th Inf Div: yellow cross.

10 40th Inf Div: brown acorn. A variant was the yellow cockerel with red comb and wattles on a black square. **11** 42nd Inf Div: red border to diamond. **12** 43rd Inf Div: dark blue square, yellow wyvern. **13** 44th Inf Div: red, sometimes with white border. **14** 45th Inf Div: khaki square, yellow drum with red top, base and diamond, dark blue square. **15** 46th Inf Div: brown trunk, green foliage edged white. Also shown on dark blue square. **16** 47th Inf Div: dark blue square, red emblem. 1944 regs give the field as black and circular. **17** 48th Inf Div: dark blue oval, blue macaw on red diamond. **18** 49th Inf Div: 1st pattern had the bear looking downwards. **19** 50th Inf Div: two red Ts. **20** 51st Inf Div: blue field, red letters and circle. **21** 52nd Inf Div: blue shield. The word MOUNTAIN in white on a blue scroll edged black was added beneath the shield later but it is doubtful if this was used on vehicles. **22** 53rd Inf Div: red W and line. **23** 54th Inf Div: red circle, blue monogram. **24** 55th Inf Div: red rose, usually on white square. **25** 56th Inf Div: red rectangle. 1st pattern used white rectangle. **26** 59th Inf Div: blue rectangle, black and red symbol. 1944 regs give a square field. **27** 61st Inf Div: red diamond, blue square. 1944 regs give a circular field. **28** 66th Inf Div: light blue triangle with yellow bar. (70th Inf Div was the 6th Inf Div renumbered in the Western Desert, and bore the sign of 6th Div.) **29** 76th Inf Div: red wherry. **30** 77th Inf Div: red sword, three wavy blue lines.

Plate V (page 17): British formation signs: Infantry.

1 78th Inf Div: yellow axe. Field was sometimes square. **2** 80th Inf Div: light blue rectangle, red ship, yellow sky. **3** 1st Indep Guards Bde: blue/red/blue field. **4** 2nd Guards Bde: blue/red/blue field. **5** 2nd Inf Bde. (5th Inf Bde used the sign of its parent div, see **Fig 26 Plate III**.) **6** 17th Inf Bde: yellow arrow head on red. Reconstruction. **7** 18th Indep Inf Bde: white bayonet and kukri edged brown on red field. **8** 23rd Bde Grp: five yellow squares on blue shield with yellow border. Reconstruction. **9** 24th Indep Guards Bde Grp: red wing on dark blue. 1944 regs give white wing in blue circle within a red star. **10** 25th Indep Inf Bde: reconstruction. **11** 27th Indep Inf Bde: blue inverted triangle on red. Reconstruction. **12** 29th Indep Inf Bde Grp. When the 36th Div was disbanded the bde used a yellow four-leafed clover above the number 29, all on a blue shield. **13** 31st Indep Bde Grp: red bull and crown detail on dark blue. **14** 32nd Indep Guards Inf Bde:

Plate III: British formation signs.

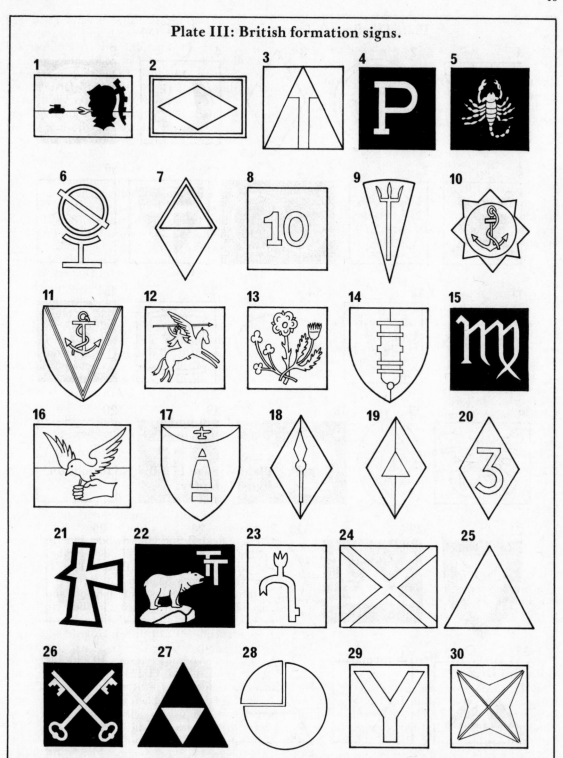

Plate IV: British formation signs; Inf Divs.

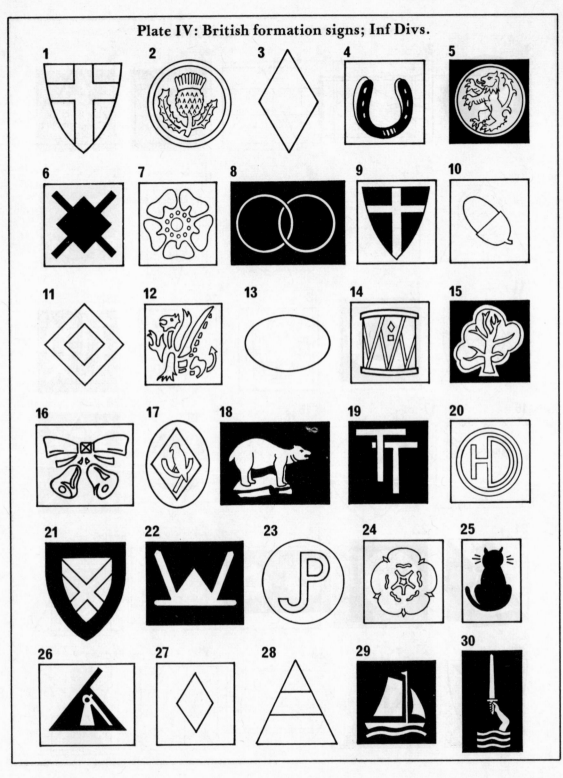

Plate V: British formation signs: Infantry.

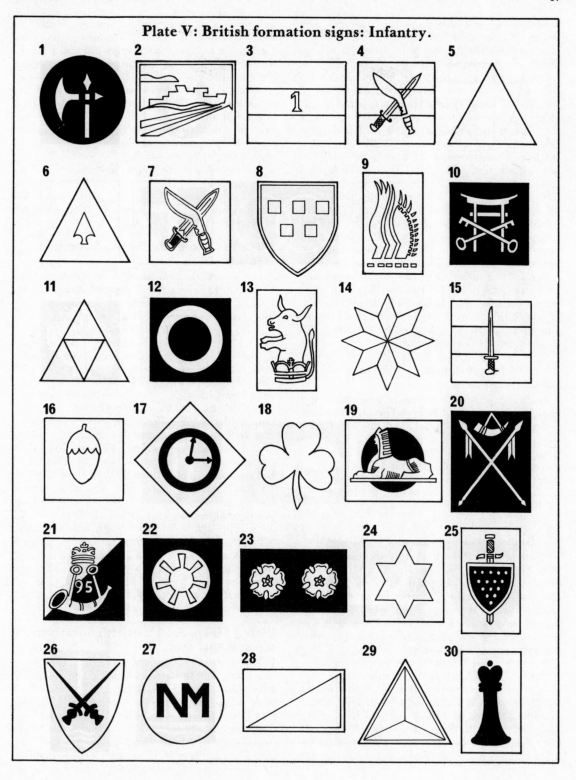

alternate red and blue diamonds, starting with red at 12 o'clock. **15** 33rd Indep Guards Inf Bde: blue/red/blue field. **16** 36th Indep Inf Bde: yellow nut, green shell, khaki square. **17** 37th Indep Inf Bde: grey diamond. **18** 38th Indep Inf Bde: green shamrock. In 1941-2, when part of 1st Div, a white spearhead was superimposed. 1944 regs give a blue crane with red head, neck and legs as the vehicle sign. **19** 56th Indep Inf Bde: yellow sphinx and rectangle. **20** 60th Indep Inf Bde: reconstruction. **21** 61st Indep Inf Bde: green/black field. **22** 70th Indep Inf Bde: red capstan on green circle. **23** 71st Indep Inf Bde: right hand rose is red. 1944 regs give green field. **24** 72nd Indep Inf Bde: red square. (72nd Inf Bde sign was red circle on black square.) **25** 73rd Indep Inf Bde: yellow roundels, border and sword hilt, on dark blue. **26** 115th Indep Inf Bde: red shield. **27** 148th Indep Inf Bde. **28** 160th Indep Inf Bde: khaki or brown rectangle bearing blue triangle. (162nd Inf Bde used the sign of its parent division, the 54th, see **Fig 23, Plate IV**.) **29** 204th Indep Inf Bde: grey (left), buff (right) and green (bottom) triangles, blue border. **30** 206th Indep Inf Bde: red rectangle.

Plate VI (opposite): British formation signs; Indep Bdes.

1 212th Indep Inf Bde: red tulip, green stalk and leaf. **2** 214th Indep Inf Bde: red on blue. **3** 218th Indep Inf Bde: yellow torch, red flame. **4** 219th Indep Inf Bde: red flames, dark blue disc with white inner border. **5** 223rd Indep Inf Bde: blue on red. **6** 231st Indep Inf Bde: red shield. **7** 301st Indep Inf Bde: dark blue on red. **8** 303rd Indep Inf Bde: red over blue rectangle. **9** 304th Indep Inf Bde: red on blue.

5   Regimental insignia

The use of regt (and lower) insignia was limited, probably because in the British Army regts became very much identified with their bdes and divs, and the formation signs of these formations were sufficient for morale purposes. Any regimental insignia carried on vehicles was therefore very much the exception rather than the rule. Some known examples are set out below.

Softskins and carriers of 1st Bn London Scottish (56th Div) had the thistle of the regt painted on the front left. Softskins and carriers of 6th Bn Yorks and Lancs Regt (46th Div) sometimes had the red and white roses of Lancashire and Yorkshire painted on the front left. In both these cases the divisional sign was painted on the front right. The 110th RAC had a green and

yellow triangle (regimental colours) painted on tank turrets and on lorries. Armoured cars of the 1st King's Dragoon Guards in Italy and northwest Europe, 1943-5, normally carried their regimental badge, a French eagle, stencilled in black on a white rectangle on both front and rear, in addition to their divisional sign. And most famous of all, the Matildas of 4th RTR serving in France in 1940 with the BEF had eyes painted on each forward side of the turret, a tradition originating in World War 1.

A number of other regimental and lower signs may be seen in **Plate III**, and there is a considerable listing of the signs used by independent RASC companies in Europe 1944-5 in **Plates VII-IX**.

Plate VII (page 20): British formation signs; RASC coys.

1 1st Coy, Army Transport (AT): red devil. **2** 1st Coy, Tank Transport (TT): red hand. **3** 2nd Coy, TT. **4** 3rd Coy, General Transport (GT): blue outline and clover leaf, yellow box. **5** 9th Coy GT: yellow beak, khaki beret. **6** No 9 Military Petrol Filling Centre: colours unknown. **7** 11th BPT Petrol Coy: yellow outlined blue, eye, nose and wheel centres also blue. **8** 13th Coy, Troop Carrying (TC): blue circle, yellow sword. **9** 14th Coy: colours unknown. **10** 15th Coy, TT. **11** 17th Coy, GT. **12** 19th Coy, GT: blue field. **13** 20th Transport Col: yellow field, blue lettering, edging and aircraft. **14** 21st Trpt Col: blue with yellow key. **15** 24th Trpt Col: white over blue, yellow bridge. **16** 25th Field Bakery: colours unknown. **17** 26th Coy, Tipper. **18** 31st Trpt Col: blue field and wick, yellow flame. **19** 32nd Trpt Col. **20** 33rd Trpt Col: yellow emblem on blue. **21** 34th Trpt Col. **22** 35th Trpt Col: yellow and black. **23** 36th Coy, AT. **24** No 36 Detail Issue Depot: colours unknown. **25** 39th Coy, GT: blue hat ribbon and coat, yellow beak and legs, holding 3rd Div sign of red on black triangle. **26** 39th Trpt Col: red outline. **27** 41st Trpt Col. **28** 43rd Trpt Col. **29** 45th Trpt Col. **30** 46th Trpt Col: blue field.

Plate VIII (page 21): British formation signs; RASC coys.

1 50th Coy, GT. **2** 75th Coy, GT: blue, red wineglass. **3** 96th Coy, TC: black and yellow. **4** 101st Coy, GT: blue beret and coat, yellow beak, hand, legs, buttons, badge and trim on coat. **5** 104th Coy, AT: flesh colour with red lips, cheek and cap, blue costume, yellow field. (106th Coy, Bridge, had the same design as 24th Trpt Col, **Fig 15, Plate VII**, but with a red bridge.) **6**

Plate VI: British formation signs; Indep Bdes.

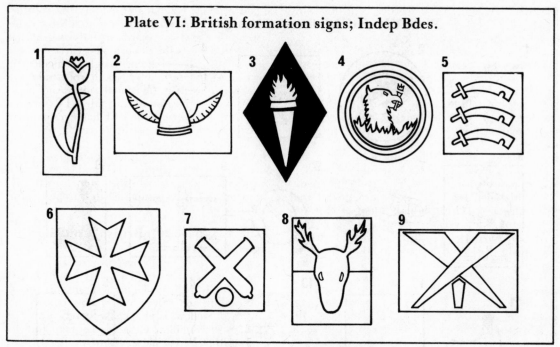

111th Coy, MAC: red snake. **7** 127th Coy, Corps Transport (CT). (128th Coy, Bridge, had same design as 24th Coy but with pale green bridge.) **8** 133rd Coy, Armoured Div Transport: yellow shell with red nose, blue wing. (147th Coy, Bridge, had the same design as 24th Coy but with a black bridge.) **9** 164th Coy, GT: blue on yellow, steering wheel rim and spokes white. **10** 168th Coy, GT: red beak, yellow pyramid, blue square. **11** 199th Coy, GT: yellow. **12** 213th Coy, GT: white cards edged blue, red diamonds. **13** 215th Coy, TC: as 43rd Coy but blue with 3 white stripes (see **Plate VII Fig 28**). **14** 234th Petrol Depot: colours unknown. **15** 236th Coy, Bridge: colours unknown. **16** 249th Coy, TC: green with purple thistle down. **17** 277th Coy, Armoured Div Trpt: colours unknown. **18** 279th Coy, AT. **19** 287th Coy, AT. **20** 288th Coy, CT: red field. **21** 299th Coy, GT: blue crown to hat, blue coat and eyes, yellow beak and legs, red cuffs, collar and handkerchief, brown cigar. **22** 311th Coy, GT: yellow arrow and border. (334th Coy, CT, used the sign of 8th Armoured Div.) **23** 372nd Coy, TT: yellow tank and figure with white belt, blue square. **24** 373rd Coy, TT. **25** 373rd Coy, TT (Middle East 1942): yellow. **26** 377th Coy, GT: yellow legs and beak. **27** 378th Coy, GT: yellow. **28** 388th Coy, TT: black and yellow tank on red diamond with white centre. **29** 401st Coy, TC. **30** 450th Coy, TT.

Plate IX (page 22): British formation signs; RASC coys.

1 451st Coy, TT. **2** 452nd Coy, TT: yellow bird, red diamond, blue beak, tail and wing tips. **3** 463rd Coy, AT: yellow half circle, blue diamond edged white. **4** 510th Coy, GT: red on white. **5** 512th Coy, AT: yellow dome, white 'reflection' on right edge, yellow elephant's head outlined in black then red, and blue/white mountains. **6** 516th Coy, GT: red hand. **7** 534th Coy, TT: colours unknown. **8** 545th Coy, TT: blue border and tank, yellow T. **9** 547th Coy, GT: black Rs on white (top left) and yellow cantons over blue. **10** 558th Coy, Water Tank: colours unknown. **11** 633rd Coy, GT: grey tyre with black and white shading, green hub with red (outer) and white nuts, yellow propeller shaded red. **12** 648th Coy AT: purple circle, green wing. (649th Coy, AT, as 648th but red wing.) **13** 701st Coy, Maintenance: blue circle, yellow aircraft. **14** 702nd Coy, Maintenance: white/yellow/blue umbrella (left to right) with white handle. **15** 705th Coy, GT: yellow mermaid, two blue waves. **16** 706th Coy, GT: blue outline and shading. **17** 710th Coy, GT. **18** 719th Coy, GT. **19** 723rd Coy, GT: green with red flower. **20** 740th Coy, Arty: blue shield, yellow sun and four rays. **21** 780th Coy, Corps HQ: red/green square, grey tyre with white centre and wing. **22** 787th Coy, GT. **23** 838th Coy, GT. **24** 840th

Plate VII: British formation signs; RASC coys.

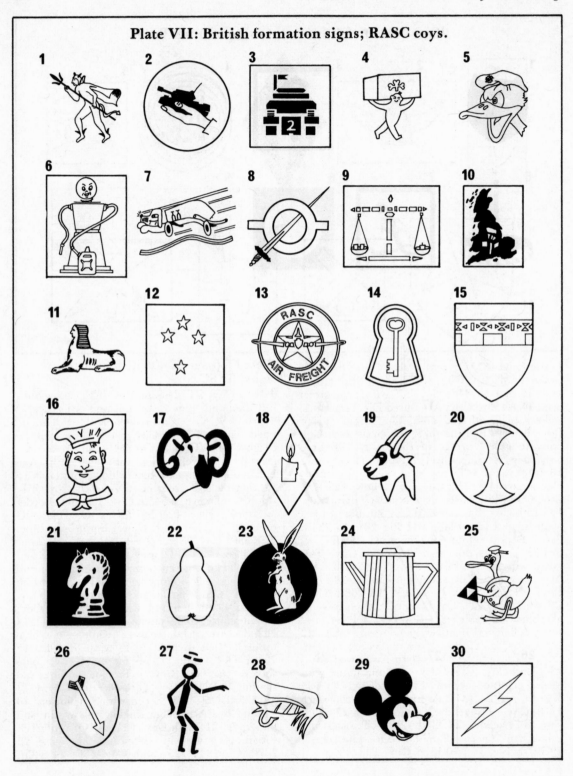

Plate VIII: British formation signs; RASC coys.

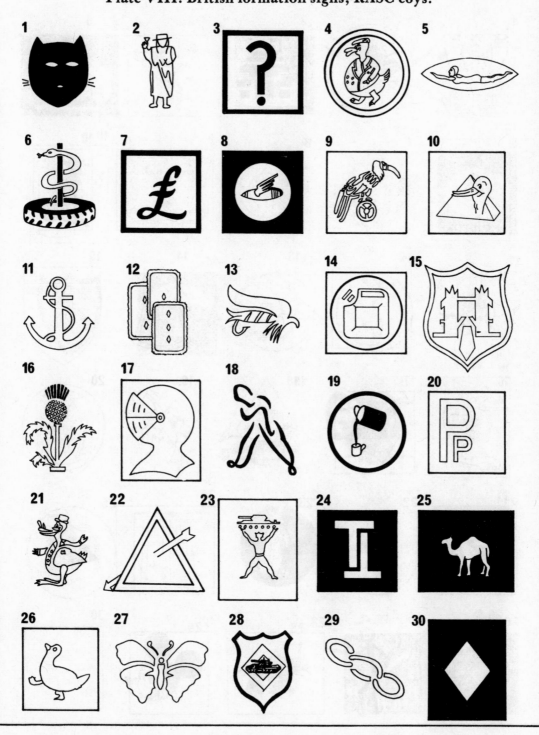

Plate IX: British formation signs; RASC coys.

Coy, GT: colours unknown. **25** 847th Coy, GT. **26** 917th Coy, GT. **27** 921st Coy, GT. **28** 1564th Coy, Arty: black on red. **29** 1572nd Coy, Arty: red horns.

6 Arm of service markings

In October 1939 a new system of unit identification was introduced which consisted of a metal plate painted in various colours to indicate the arm of service to which the vehicle belonged, and bearing a code number to indicate unit identity. Official instructions concerning these markings, known as arm of service flash and unit serial number, were virtually unchanged during the war, and therefore I quote in detail from the 1943 vehicle markings pamphlet:

'Unit vehicles will bear two signs stencilled on the vehicles, one facing the front and one the rear. The signs will be, approximately, 9½ by 8½ in (24.1 by 21.6 cm). The position of the signs will differ with varying types of vehicles and cannot be standardised but will, where possible, be on the off-side front mudguard or some similar position to the front, and on the off-side of the tailboard, or some similar position to the rear. The serial number allotted to the unit will be painted in white and as large as possible on the coloured background:

'On motor cycles and motor cycle combinations the unit sign will be painted on each forward end of the petrol tank and on the rear mudguard.

'Unit signs will not be painted on, or fitted to, trailers.

'To distinguish GHQ command and corps troops from divisional units and to distinguish AA Command and Home Guard vehicles, signs will be marked as follows:

Corps Troops: White horizontal 2 in (5.1 cm) bar above the serial number.

GHQ Troops and command troops: White horizontal 2 in (5.1 cm) bar below serial number.

'In the case of passenger-carrying vehicles in transport coys, RASC, the signs will be double the height specified for unit signs: the lower half will bear the sign and colours of the unit upon whose charge the vehicles are held, and the upper half will be painted black. When such units are carrying personnel the serial number of the embussed unit will be displayed in white chalk on the upper half of the sign, thereby showing both serial numbers. The signs will be stencilled on the off-side front cab panel (in the case of the QL Bedford troop-carrying vehicle the lamp bracket plate will be removed and the bolts replaced to fill the holes) and on the near-side of the tailboard or rear panel.'

Vehicle instructions issued prior to 1943 stipulate that removable metal plates should be used to carry these signs, and that the reverse of the plate should be painted khaki and bear the word PASS in white. The intention was that any vehicle unable to continue on a march for any reason could display the PASS sign to prevent unnecessary hold-ups. These plates had been phased out by 1943, and thereafter almost all signs were stencilled directly on to the vehicles. AFVs normally had the signs placed as per instructions, but sometimes bore them on the lower surface of the glacis.

The arm of service colours of the Royal Signals (white and blue) prevented the use of white paint for the serial number or for any 2 in (5.1 cm) bar used to distinguish higher echelon troops. The 1942 regulations therefore stipulated that red paint be used for these on Royal Signals flashes. Although this exception to the rule was not repeated in the 1943 regulations, Signals units used red numbers and bars from at least 1942 onwards.

In the RASC independent companies it was quite common practice to use the upper half of the sign to display permanently their coy insignia instead of the chalked serial number of embussed units.

The arm of service colours were designated by War Office letter, not the vehicle markings pamphlets. Although this writer has not yet seen all these letters (they were released in 1972 and subsequently passed to the Public Records Office for sorting and filing) most of the colours used are well known, often being linked to regt or corps colours. However, there are a number of discrepancies in the early war years, which may be due to error on the part of the units, or variations introduced in the interests of security.

The divs of the basic square sign are illustrated in **Plate X, Figs 1-15.** The colours for the various arms are set out below: Armoured recce regts: **Fig 2**, green over blue. Armoured car regts: **Fig 2**, green over white. Airborne units: **Fig 1**, maroon, with light blue serial number. (These units also used infantry arm of service flashes). Senior Inf Bde in Inf Divisions, or senior armoured regt in Armoured Divisions, or Inf units in Indep Inf Bdes: **Fig 1**, red. 2nd Inf Bde in Inf Div, RAC Training units: **Fig 1**, green. Junior Inf Bde in Inf Div, tanks of Armoured Bde of mixed div (1942): **Fig 1**, brown. Royal Engineers: **Fig 1**, blue. REME: **Fig 3**, blue/yellow/red (from October 1943 at the

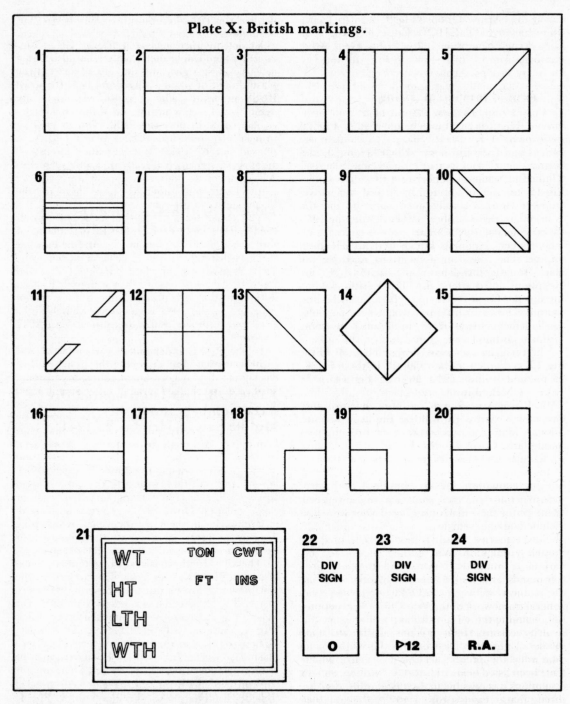

Plate X: British markings.

earliest). Royal Arty: **Fig 2**, red/blue. RAOC: **Fig 4**, blue/red/blue (from October 1943 at earliest). RASC: **Fig 5**, red/green. Royal Signals: **Fig 2**, white over blue (from October 1943). Air Liason Sections: **Fig 7**, red/blue. Royal Marines: **Fig 6**, from top to bottom, blue, yellow, green, red, blue; north-west Europe, 1944-5. Corps Troops: **Fig 8**, 2 in (5.1 cm) white bar at top. Army Troops: **Fig 9**, 2 in (5.1 cm) white bar at base. GHQ Troops: **Fig 10**, 2 in (5.1 cm) white bar diagonally, with gap for serial number, from October 1943, before this date as for Army Troops. Army Group: **Fig 11**, 2 in (5.1 cm) bar diagonally, with gap for serial number, from October 1943, before this date as for Army Troops. Home Defence Bns: **Fig 2**, red over brown, UK 1941. Young Soldier Bns: **Fig 7**, red/brown, UK 1941. War Office Schools, Depots and Establishments: **Fig 12**, top left and bottom right black, other two quarters white. Command Schools, Depots and Establishments: **Fig 12**, top left and bottom right red, other two quarters white.

Prior to the October 1943 regulations the Royal Signals, RAOC and armoured regts in independent armoured bdes, used an all black square. The following formations used an all black square throughout the war (with the exceptions noted after): RAMC, RAPC, CMP, Intelligence Corps, formation HQs, and all other units not having a colour of their own (mainly small detachments such as bath units, hygiene sections, postal service, etc).

Variants known to have existed are: RASC: **Fig 13**, red/green, BEF 1939-40. RASC: **Fig 4**, yellow/blue/yellow, 1940. RASC: **Fig 14**, red/green. CMP: **Fig 4**, red/black/red, January 1945. Royal Arty: **Fig 5**, red/blue, Fortress and Coast Arty. Army Tank Bdes: **Fig 2**, in various colours, blue over red, green over brown, blue over yellow. Corps Troops: **Fig 15**, 2 in (5.1 cm) white bar set a small distance down from the top of the square, early war years (in fact a literal interpretation of the 1943 regulations).

Instructions on the allocation of unit serial numbers for these arm of service flashes were not included in the vehicle markings pamphlet for obvious security reasons, but were issued in limited circulation War Office letters to the various commands. Individual theatres and commands also issued separate instructions on the subject between 1939-43, following the general framework of the War Office instructions but changing the serial numbers as necessary for security reasons. Hence it is not possible to list all the serial numbers used during the war, not to guarantee the precise accuracy of those which have been listed below. However, with only a few exceptions it is possible to divide all numbers into three main categories: 1-100 for units at divisional level, 100-1,000 for units at Army level, and 1,000 upwards for units at Army Group level. Most known serial numbers have been gleaned from the War Office letters and

pictorial sources, but it must be remembered that even these numbers would have been changed after an unknown period of usage, partly to confuse the enemy and partly because of the changes within divisional organisation. **Tables 2-7** illustrate the basic system of arm of service flashes and unit serial numbers: a listing of all known numbers for north-west Europe, 1944-5, is given in Peter Hodge's book, *British Military Markings*.

Plate X (opposite): British markings.
See text.

Table 2: British Armoured Div serial numbers and flashes 1939-40.

Unit	Europe	Middle East
Armoured car regt		14 White/green (?)
Armoured Bde HQ	3 Green	23 (?) Red
3 Armoured Regts	4 5 6 Green	24 25 26 Red
Armoured Bde HQ	7 Green	27 (?) Green
3 Armoured Regts	8 9 10 Green	28 29 30 Green
RHA Regt	11 Red/blue	?
LAA/A/T Regt	12 Red/blue	?
2 Motor Bns	13 14 Red	?
2 LAD with Motor Bns	13 14 Black	?

Table 3: British 1st Armoured Div serial numbers and flashes, Middle East, November 22 1941.

Unit	Serial	Flash
Div HQ	99	Black
Employ Platoon	62	Black
HQ 2nd Armoured Bde	71	Red
Queen's Bays	40	Red
9th Lancers	86	Red
10th Hussars	67	Red
1st Rifle Bde	60	Red
Light repair section	57	Red
Recovery section	72	Red
Ordnance Field Park sec	38	Red
HQ 22nd Armoured Bde	49	Green
2nd Royal Glos Hussars	65	Green
3rd County of London Yeomanry	68	Green
4th County of London Yeomanry	83	Green
2nd KRRC	87	Green
Light repair section	69	Green
Recovery section	35	Green
Ordnance Field Park sec	42	Green
HQ Support Grp	84	Brown
11th HAC	77	Red/blue
61 LAA Regt	54	Red/blue
76 A/T Regt	55	Red/blue
Light repair section	91	Brown
Recovery section	94	Brown

Ordnance Field Park sec	37	Brown
12th Lancers	76	Green/blue
HQ RE	59	Blue
1 Field Sqdn	33	Blue
7 Field Sqdn	22	Blue
1 Field Park Sqdn	50	Blue
HQ RASC	47	Red/green
2 Armoured Bde Coy	82	Red/green
22 Armoured Bde Coy	78	Red/green
Support Grp Coy	75	Red/green
Div Troops Coy	80	Red/green
1 Tank Transporter Coy	96	Red/green
2 Tank Transporter Coy	25	Red/green
1 Armoured Div Workshop RAOC	31	Black
Div Ord, Field Park RAOC	70	Black
3 Light Field Ambulance	52, 27, 58	Black
Field Hygiene Section	45	Black
Mobile Bath unit	95	Black
Provost Coy	79	Black
Field Postal Unit	66	Black

Table 4: Serial numbers and flashes for armoured divs, north-west Europe, 1944-5.

Unit	Serial	Flash
Div HQ	40	Black
REME HQ	40	Blue/yellow/red
RASC HQ	80	Red/green
RA HQ	40	Red/blue
Armoured Recce Regt	45	Green/blue
Armoured car Regt (Corps Troops)	44	Green/blue
Armoured Bde HQ	50	Red
3 Armoured Regts	51 52 53	Red
Motor Bn	54	Red
Inf Bde HQ	60	Green
3 Inf Bns	61 62 63	Green
Independent Machine-Gun Coy	64	Black
2 Field Regts RA	74 76	Red/blue
Anti-Tank Regt	77	Red/blue
Light AA Regt	73	Red/blue
2 Field Sqdns RE	41 46	Blue
Field Park Sqdn RE	42	Blue
Div Bridging Troop	52	Blue
Armoured Bde Coy RASC	81	Red/green
Inf Bde Coy RASC	83	Red/green
Div Troops Coy RASC	84	Red/green
Transport Coy RASC	82	Red/green
Ordnance Field Park	97	Blue/red/blue
Armoured Bde Workshop REME	99	Blue/yellow/red
Inf Bde Workshop REME	100	Blue/yellow/red
Light AA Regt Workshop REME	73	Blue/yellow/red
Div Signals	—*	White/blue

*Signals adopt the number of unit to which they have been attached.

Light Field Ambulance	89	Black
Field Ambulance	90	Black
Field Dressing Station	93	Black

Table 5: British Inf Div serial numbers and flashes, 1939-40, Europe.

Unit	Serial	Flash
Div HQ	1	Black
Inf Bde HQ		Red
3 Inf Bns	14 15 16	Red
Inf Bde HQ		Green
3 Inf Bns	17 18 19	Green
Inf Bde HQ		Brown
3 Inf Bns	20 21 22	Brown
A/T Coy	73	
Cav Regt	2	Green
LAD	2	Black
Field Park Coy RE	33	Blue
Ammo Coy RASC	23	Red/green
Supply Coln RASC	24	Red/green
Petrol Coy RASC	25	Red/green
Field Regt RA*	10	Red/blue
Field Regt RA*	11	Red/blue
Field Regt RA*	12	Red/blue
A/T Regt*	13	Red/blue

*LADs with each regt used same serial number on black flash.

Table 6: British Inf Div serial numbers and flashes 1940-2.

Unit	UK	Middle East
Div HQ	40 Black	50 Black
HQ Inf Bde	81 Red	65 Red
3 Inf Bns	55 56 57 Red	91 80 52 Red
HQ Inf Bde	87 Green	72 Green
3 Inf Bns	60 61 62 Green	84 75 92 Green
HQ Inf Bde	94 Brown	58 Brown
3 Inf Bns	67 68 69 Brown	60 62 89 Brown
MG Bn	53 Red	51 Red
Armoured car Regt	41 Blue/green	81 Blue/green
HQ Div Arty	40 Red/blue	82 Red/blue
A/T Regt	46 Red/blue	96 Red/blue
3 Field Regts RA	42 43 44 Red/blue	88 71 53 Red/blue
LAA Regt	47 Red/blue	55 Red/blue
HQ RE	40 Blue	63 Blue
3 Field Coys RE	49 50 51 Blue	78 70 57 Blue
Field Park Coy	48 Blue	59 Blue
Div Signals	52 White/blue	?
HQ RASC	40 Red/green	67 Red/green
3 RASC Coys	70 71 72 Red/green	69 74 95 48 Red/green
Workshop Coy	84 Black	15 35 76 Black
3 Light Ambul Coys	75 76 77 Black	99 54 86 Black
Field Postal unit	80 Black	97 Blue
Provost unit	79 Black	68 Black
Hygiene section	—	61 Black

Serial numbers and flashes were the same for 1942-5, European theatre, except for the following minor differences:

MG Bn	64	Black
Div Bridging P1	52	Blue
3 Inf Bde Coys RASC	70 71 73	Red/green
Div Troops Coy RASC	72	Red/green
Ordnance Field Park	92	Blue/red/blue
3 Inf Bde Workshops	88 89 90	Blue/yellow/red
LAA Regt Workshop	47	Blue/yellow/red
2 Field Dressing Sta	82 83	Black

Signals adopted number of unit to which they had been attached.

Table 7: Serial numbers and flashes for British Airborne Forces, 1944-5.

Unit	Serial	Flash
Div HQ and Def P1	40	Black
Indep Para Coy	50	Black
HQ Para Bde and Def P1	81	Red
3 Para Bns	55 56 57	Red
HQ Para Bde and Def Pl	87	Green
3 Para Bns	60 61 62	Green
HQ A/Ldg Bde and Def Pl	94	Brown
3 A/Ldg Bns	67 68 69	Brown
Armoured Recce Regt	85 or 41	See note
HQ Div RA	40	Red/blue
A/Ldg Light Regt RA	46	Red/blue
A/Ldg A/T Regt	47	Red/blue
HQ Div RE	40	Blue
2 Para Sqdns RE Field Coy	48 ?	Blue
Field Park Coy	49	Blue
Div Signals	40	White/blue
HQ RASC	40	Red/green
3 Light Coys RASC	70 71 73	Red/green
2 Field Ambl	75 76	Black
A/Ldg Field Ambl	77	Black
Div RAOC	92	Blue/red/blue
HQ REME	40	Blue/yellow/red
Workshop	40	Blue/yellow/red
5 A/Ldg LAD	47 81 87 94 85	Blue/yellow/red
Provost Coy	79	Black
Postal unit	80	Black
HQ Indep Para Bde	109	Black
3 Para Bns	110 111 112	Maroon
HQ 1st Airborne Corps	17	Black with white bar at top

Note: 1st AB Div's 1 A/Ldg Recce Sqdn used 41 on green/blue. 6th AB Div's 6 AB Div Armoured Recce Sqdn used 85 on maroon. Serial numbers were usually in light blue, with possible exceptions of RE and Signals units, and A/Ldg Bde. Some Para Bns used what appears to be the Bn number on the formation sign, just beneath the front hooves of Pegasus.

7 Tactical markings

The War Office instructions on tactical markings are, as usual, quite explicit:

'Tactical signs may be placed on vehicles at the discretion of regimental, etc, commanders, subject to any orders as to standardisation that higher command may impose. Such signs, if placed on the front or rear of the vehicle, must be limited to one in front and one in rear, and must not interfere with any of the signs mentioned above. Tactical signs on the sides of vehicles are preferable except in armoured formations. Corps, div, bde or btty, etc, numbers and regt crests or titles cannot be permitted except for training establishments, certain fixed administrative units, bomb disposal units, traffic control units and Home Guard units, who will make use of abbreviated titles.

'In armoured formations and units, tactical signs will be painted on the front, sides and rear of the turret of AFVs and on the front, sides and rear of B vehicles and such A vehicles as have no turret.'

Details of the tactical signs to be used were listed separately in a War Office letter, which was classified as secret. However, the signs were well known during the war. For AFVs they were geometrical shapes, painted in thick outline with the colour of the vehicle showing in the centre: a diamond for HQ Sqdn, triangle for A Sqdn, square for B Sqdn, circle for C Sqdn, and a solid rectangle painted vertically for a D Sqdn if it existed. Officially these emblems were to be red for the senior armoured regt within an armoured bde, then yellow, with blue for the junior regt. If a fourth regt existed, it used green. Independent regts used white. In fact this system was not always adhered to, possibly because of regts being moved from one bde to another. In addition, the signs were not positioned as instructions, normally being limited to vehicle or turret sides only, though occasionally they were repeated on turret rear and tailboards. The troop within a sqdn was indicated by the troop number (HQ, 1 to 4) usually painted inside the sqdn sign, though in some regts it was painted alongside the sign. The tanks of the SHQ and RHQ fighting troops sometimes had individual vehicles identified by initials instead of using HQ, thus CO, 2I/C, etc. A solid white oblong painted horizontally was added to these signs as a tactical marking for the support company of the Lorried Inf Bn in an armoured div in the early war years.

Vehicles belonging to the Long Range Desert Group used an individual system, a black square painted on both front and rear mudguards, and bearing in white a letter to indicate patrol, with below it a number for the vehicle within that patrol; for example, $\frac{R}{4}$ 4th vehicle of R (New Zealand) Patrol, B Troop, and $\frac{T}{9}$ 9th vehicle of T (New Zealand) Patrol, C Troop.

Traffic Control vehicles were marked with the letters TC in white on a black background.

Bomb Disposal vehicles had their mudguards painted signal red and had the letters BDS in red painted in 4 in (10.2 cm) high capitals on some part of the front of the vehicle other than the windscreen.

All softskins were also supposed to have the letter B, or RASC if belonging to that corps, painted in white, 2 in high (5.1 cm) on both sides and rear, according to the 1940-3 regulations, but in fact this practice was mostly discontinued in the early years of the war. It was also quite common for the vehicles within an RASC general transport company to be identified by numerals or letters, or both. These were painted in any convenient, prominent position.

The Royal Arty employed a distinctive system of tactical markings based on the regt's arm of service colours: the system was used throughout the war. **Figs 16-20** in **Plate X** illustrate the 8 in (20.3 cm) square red/blue backgrounds for the tactical letters and numbers: **Fig 16**, RHQ, red over blue; **Fig 17**, 1st or P Btty, red square on blue field; **Fig 18**, 2nd or Q Btty; **Fig 19**, 3rd or R Btty; **Fig 20**, 4th or S Btty (where applicable). Note the red square is moved in a clockwise direction to indicate btty number.

A white letter or letters were superimposed on the blue fields to identify individual vehicles within each battery. These letters and their meanings are shown in **Table 8**. (There were two troops in each battery; AB, CD, EF). If a number was added to the vehicle letter, this represented the individual gun within a troop, though examples of this are rare. In SP regts equipped with Priests in 1944-5, letters were sometimes used instead, thus giving A Troop, for example, AA, AB, AC, AD. The vehicles of the OP parties were marked RA1, RA2, etc, for A Troop, RB1, RB2, etc, for B Troop, and so on.

These signs normally appeared on the front of vehicles, and were sometimes repeated on cab doors. Where no suitable surface existed at the front, a metal plate was used, often attached to the radiator.

Survey Regts used the RA system, but the RHQ sign had a yellow square in the top right hand corner, and the squares on the btty signs

were yellow instead of red.

Vehicles belonging to the Royal Marine Armoured Support Groups, employed in the initial assault during the invasion of France in June 1944, used their arm of service flash with the btty number (1 to 5) painted in white so that it spanned all five sections of that flash. The sign appeared on AFV hulls at front and rear. Each btty consisted of four troops, identified by the first letter of the vehicle's name: see section 9 below.

Table 8: Royal Artillery tactical signs.

Vehicle	Tactical sign
Regt Cmdrs	Z
2 i/c	Z2
Adjutant	A1
RSM	A2
Regt Signals	M
Bn Cmdrs	X
2 i/c	X2
Gun Position Officer	G
'A' Troop GPO	GA (B Troop GB etc)
Bn Command Post, Captain	K (K1, K2 etc)
CP Officer	H
Assistant CPO	Y
Troop Cmdrs	R
'A' Troop Cmdrs	RA (B Troop RB etc)
Troop Leader	TL
'A' Troop Leader	TLA (B Troop TLB etc)
Gun tractors of 'A' Troop	A1 to A4
Ammunition tractors of 'A' Troop	A5, A6 etc
Signals Officer	S1
Signals Section	S
Survey Officer	SVR1
'B' Echelon	Q

---

8   Call signs

There was a shortage of wirelesses in the early war years but by 1944 almost all AFVs and many other vehicles were fitted with a wireless set and had a number, a call sign, which was used to identify them on the air. These numbers were obviously a useful method of identifying the vehicles themselves, and in the last year of the war were sometimes painted on AFVs to enable troop and sqdn leaders to identify and control swiftly in combat conditions the individual vehicles within their unit. The numbers were painted in white, usually solid but on rare occasions in outline only or in red outlined with white, in large Arabic numerals on the AFV's rear, and were usually repeated on the sides in a much smaller size. They were often placed within the sqdn symbol and included the troop number, for example, 1 for 1st Troop Leader, 1A for 1st Troop Sergeant, 1B for 1st Troop Corporal, all within the sqdn's symbol. When a fourth tank was added to troops in late 1944, then the letter C was used.

It was normal for the call signs to be used only at a sqdn level, so numbers higher than four did not occur: in some regts call signs were not used at all as tactical markings, identification being by names alone. However, occasionally two-digit numbers do occur in war-time photographs: it is believed these were allotted as in the post-war system, and therefore a full network of these call signs is listed below to assist in the identification of vehicles carrying such numbers.

At a regimental level, numbers 1-20 were allocated to RHQ Sqdn and rear link vehicles. A Sqdn used its normal numbers but added 20 (thus 1st Troop's 1 became 21, 21A, 21B, 21C), B Sqdn added 40, C Sqdn added 60, and the Recce Troop added 80. 1-4 rear link vehicles for A, B and C Sqdns and Recce Troop respectively. 6 bulldozers*. 5 and 7 spare for attached troops. 8 and 8A HQ fighting vehicles*. 9 CO's Jeep or similar vehicle*. 10A link to A echelon. 10B link to B echelon. 11 2I/C's tank*. 12 REME*. 12A AQMS*. 12B Recovery*. (At sqdn level these were usually only 12A and 12B, half-tracks or similar vehicles used by REME fitters attached to each sqdn.) 13 Communications Troop. 14 Technical Adjutant. 15 Signals Officer. 16 Medical Officer. 17 Adjutant. 17A Intelligence Officer. 18 Liason Officer*. 21, 21A, 21B, 21C 1st Troop, A Sqdn. 22, 22A, 22B, 22C 2nd Troop, A Sqdn. 23, 23A 23B, 23C 3rd Troop, A Sqdn. 24, 24A, 24B, 24C 4th Troop, A Sqdn. 41-41C 1st Troop, B Sqdn. 42-42C 2nd Troop, B Sqdn. 43-43C 3rd Troop, B Sqdn. 44-44C 4th Troop, B Sqdn. 61-61C 1st Troop, C Sqdn. 62-62C 2nd Troop, C Sqdn. 63-63C 3rd Troop, C Sqdn. 64-64C 4th Troop, C Sqdn. 81-81A, 82-82A, 83-83A, 84-84A Recce Troop. 96 Arty liason, 96A, 96B, 96C being observers' tanks with the sqdns. 97 RE (if attached). 97A, 97B, 97C various specialised armoured vehicles RE if attached. 99 Infantry Liason Officer. 99A, 99B, 99C Infantry Liason Officers with the sqdns.

9 Vehicle names

The official instructions stipulate only:

'Names may be painted on A vehicles provided that they do not disclose the identity of the unit or interfere with other markings.'

Add 20, 40 or 60 when attached to each sqdn.

In fact vehicle names were a popular form of tactical marking, particularly in the RTRs where a tradition existed of identifying AFVs by names rather than numbers or letters, a tradition certainly known to the enemy. B.T. White has listed British tank names at length in his book on the subject, and it would be futile to do more than summarise the subject here when such an excellent source already exists. Suffice to say that the RTR regts usually used names beginning with the letter which corresponded to their number, ie, 3rd RTR used C, 4th RTR D, 5th RTR E, etc, (1st RTR only used the letter A in the early war years: there is no information on 2nd RTR), while TA bns of the RTR, which were numbered from 40th upwards, used the names of ships or famous Admirals and the like. Cavalry regts often used the names of famous horses, races, hunts and so on, while the Yeomanry often used names of local origin, the Sherwood Foresters, for example, choosing such obvious names as Robin Hood, Little John, and others. In the 1st and 2nd Household Cav Regts, the names were linked to the sqdn: in the 2nd Regt, for example, there was Aden in A Sqdn, Bacchus in B Sqdn, and so on. The same system was often employed in some RAC regts, while others used names beginning with a letter which linked them to their Infantry origin, for example, Churchills of 144th RAC (formerly the East Lancs Regt) had names beginning with E.

In the London Scottish in 1945 the carriers bore names beginning with letters related to their roles: names such as Fife Forfar and Forres for flame-thrower carriers; anti-tank carriers had names beginning with A; mortar carriers had names beginning with M; and MMG carriers the letter M but with a second word, ie, Murray Field.

Tanks of the Royal Marine Support Groups also used names to identify individual vehicles within the btties, for example, Hunter, Fox (both H Troop, 2nd Btty), Seawolf (S Troop, 5th Btty), and Vidette (5th Btty, troop unknown). Names were usually painted on the front lower hull and turret rear or sides. White paint was normally used, but various colours could crop up, 141st RAC using light blue, and 161st RAC yellow on black, for example.

10 Vehicle serial numbers

Sometime prior to World War 2 a serial number system had been introduced whereby the year of the vehicle's issue was indicated by the first two digits of the number, thus 37 . . ., 38 . . ., 39 . . . .

This system was abandoned in the early years of the war, possibly in 1942, probably because of the vast expansion in vehicle production, and thereafter four- to seven-digit numbers were used to indicate the sequence in which the vehicle was taken into Army service.

These numbers were preceded by a letter which indicated vehicle type: A ambulances, C motor cycles, including motor cycle combinations, F armoured cars and some scout cars, H wheeled tractors, L lorries (over 15 cwt), M cars and some scout cars, T tanks and carriers, V vans, X trailers, Z trucks (15 cwt and under). During the course of the war several new prefixes were introduced: E engineer vehicles (limited to some bulldozers and earth-moving equipment), P amphibious vehicles, S SP guns and some other variants on tank hulls. In addition, Centaur and Cavalier tanks with Liberty or Meteor engines had the prefix L or M, and some re-worked Churchills had the prefix W.

Number and prefix were stencilled on both sides of the bonnet and on the tailboard of softskins, though in many examples the number appeared on cab doors instead, particularly in the case of the heavier lorries lacking a bonnet as such. AFVs usually carried their numbers on the hull sides, but early in the war they were sometimes painted on the forward edge of the glacis. As with the softskins, position was mainly dictated by surfaces available, thus Shermans nearly always had their numbers on the hull side towards the rear, as did Churchills.

The numbers and prefixes were normally painted in white, but light blue paint was used on Airborne vehicles, and black paint on vehicles in desert camouflage paint. Stencils were normally employed, the letters and numbers standing 3½ in (8.9 cm) high by 2 in (5.1 cm) wide. Motor cycles carried half-size numbers on each side of the petrol tank or on plates on front and rear mudguards.

Vehicles in the Middle East did not carry the normal prefixes prior to 1941, but instead had a WD suffix. During this early period the serial numbers were normally repeated in Arabic characters on the right-hand half of the number plate, which was carried at front and rear in the manner of civilian number plates. In India, Burma and the Far East, the Indian Army system was adopted: see under India, section 10.

Before the war civilian number plates were carried on all Army vehicles in addition to their Army serial number and many of these plates continued to appear on vehicles as late as the winter of 1940-1. Many vehicles, including tanks, belonging to the BEF carried these plates in France in 1940. They were secured front and back and had white letters and numbers on a black background.

11   Bridge classification numbers

From 1939 onwards the Army had a system for ensuring that bridges would not be used by vehicles which were too heavy for them. This system was administered by the Royal Engineers, whose duty it was to ensure that all bridges were marked with a bridge class number, painted in black on a 16 in diameter (45.2 cm) circular yellow field and placed about ten yards (9.14 m) each side of the bridge on the approach roads. Bridge class numbers were assigned to all types of vehicles, and if a vehicle's class number was less than or equal to the class number of the bridge, then it could cross the bridge. If its class number was higher than that of the bridge, then it was diverted to a stronger bridge. This system was employed particularly in the Italian and north-west European campaigns, where it was also adopted by the US Army. It was used for temporary bridges erected by Army engineers as well as for civilian bridges.

The 1943 vehicle markings pamphlet has no less than 36 pages listing the bridge class numbers for every conceivable mark of vehicle. Obviously it is not possible to reproduce the list here, while to confuse matters many war-time photographs actually show vehicles bearing different class numbers to those listed, but the following list does give a selection of the class numbers for vehicles most likely to be found in combat units.

Class 1: 2-3-seater cars, small trailers. *Class 2:* 2-7-seater cars, 8 cwt trucks, 15 cwt trailers. *Class 3:* heavy cars, bren and scout carriers, Jeeps, light recce cars and ambulances, some 2-ton, four-wheeled trailers, some 15 cwt trucks. *Class 4:* Dingo and Humber scout cars, light ambulances, some 15 cwt trucks. *Class 5:* most 15 cwt trucks, some 30 cwt lorries, White scout cars, ambulances, Humber staff car, universal carriers. (Jeeps also appear with this number in many photographs). *Class 6:* most 30 cwt lorries, some 3-tonners, Quad tractors. *Class 7:* some 3-tonners, Daimler and Humber armoured cars, Tetrarch Light tank. *Class 8:* 3-tonners, M14 half tracks, White 15 cwt half track. *Class 9:* Dukws, some 3-tonners, including most 6 × 4 and 6 × 6. (Daimler armoured cars and Quads also appear with this number in many photographs.) *Class 10:* 7-ton, six-wheeled light recovery trailers, AEC 6-ton lorry, some 6 × 4 3-tonners. *Class 11:* Diamond T 4-ton trucks. *Class 12:* AEC Matador, AEC Dorchester ACV, 5-6-ton 4 × 2 lorries. *Class 14:* AEC armoured car, A13 Cruiser tank, 6-tonners 6 × 4. *Class 15:* Stuart/ Honey tank, Staghound armoured car, (AEC Matadors also appear with this number in many photographs). *Class 16:* Valentine tank. *Class 17:* 6-tonners 6 × 6. *Class 18:* Valentine bridgelayer, Diamond T tank transporter tractor. *Class 24:* Matilda tank. *Class 30:* Cromwell tank, Sexton, Ram, M10, Sherman tank. (Shermans also appear in many photographs with the Class 33.) *Class 40:* Churchill tanks.

The class numbers were in black, usually on a yellow disc 9 in (22.8 cm) in diameter, though on many front line AFVs the disc was omitted, the number being surrounded instead by a yellow circle and occasionally outlined in yellow. In North Africa, because of the camouflage paint used, the yellow disc was usually omitted completely, a black circle being stencilled round the number on occasions in its place. The signs were carried on the off-side front of vehicles, usually painted directly on to the vehicle, though where this was not possible a circular metal plate was used, often fastened to the radiators of the heavier softskins.

When a vehicle had a trailer, it carried two numbers on its bridge class plate, the upper one representing the towing vehicle and trailer, the bottom one the towing vehicle without the trailer. They were separated by a black horizontal bar. The numbers on the trailer were the tow and trailer combined over the trailer class number: the latter was always shown in larger numerals. On tank transporters the top class number represented the tractor, trailer and load, while the bottom number represented the tractor only. On the trailer the top figure represented the trailer and load, the bottom figure the trailer only. Thus a Diamond T tank transporter had the bridge class $\frac{70}{18}$, an AEC Matador towing a 6 pdr gun had $\frac{18}{12}$, towing a trailer $\frac{6}{10}$, a Quad towing a 25 pdr gun had $\frac{8}{6}$, and a Jeep with a trailer $\frac{2}{3}$.

12   Shipping and rail loading marks

Mobilisation numbers, consisting of five or, more usually, six digits, were allocated to vehicles when mobilising for shipment overseas, and these were positioned on the front of the vehicle, either chalked or painted roughly in white. The numbers were normally only carried on the vehicles for the brief period prior to embarkation, on the voyage, and for another brief period after landing. Some examples are: 1874 4th RTR, France, 1940. 1875 7th RTR, Normandy, 1944. 16005 HQ 21st Tank Bde. 17485 carrier, France, 1940. 19013 Staffs Yeomanry. 24229 North Irish Horse. 30356 HQ 6th Assault Regt, RE, 1944. 31862 HQ Guards Armoured Div. 37105 1st Assault Sqdn RAC, 1944. 50581 102nd RTR.

Sometimes the mobilisation number had added above or below it the number and type of landing craft in which the vehicle was to travel, for example, 16000 LST 368 (Sherman, 1944) and 33214 LST 3113 (Dukw, 1944). Roman numerals were occasionally used in this context, thus 383/8/211/LCTIV (Sherman BAFV just before D Day).

On occasions, particularly for the BEF movement in 1939, mobilisation flashes, such as were normally painted on kit bags, were also used on vehicles. These were rectangular in shape, and BEF vehicles had the rectangle divided horizontally into three equal sections, coloured red/yellow/red, blue/green/blue, white/ yellow/white, or all yellow. The flashes were painted below the mobilisation number. Some examples of combined numbers and flashes are 19013 over white and yellow, 24229 over red/ yellow/red, 50581 over all green. (See numbers listed above for unit identity.) The significance of these numbers and flashes was known only to the staff of Movement Control.

Details of vehicle size and weight were carried on a standard black square panel which could be stuck on a vehicle, the necessary information then being chalked on: see **Fig 21** on **Plate X**. The panel had a narrow white border, and the pre-marked abbreviations were also in white. This panel was employed on vehicles involved in the major landings in the Italian and north-west European campaigns.

When vehicles were to be shipped by aircraft, a vertical yellow line not exceeding 6 in (15.2 cm) in length and ¾ in (20 mm) wide (½ in/13 mm in the case of motor cycles) was painted on the near- side of the vehicle in such a position as not to become obscured by covers, etc. The precise locations were set out in a special leaflet, and represented the precise point of balance. The regulations applied only to motor cycles, 5 cwt cars or Jeeps, 15 cwt 4 × 2 trucks, GS Ford and Morris, airborne trailers, GS 10 cwt two-wheel trailers, and two-wheel, 180-gallon water trailers. See **Plate XI** for examples.

Plate XI (below): British markings for shipment in aircraft.
1 10 cwt two-wheeled GS trailer. **2** Willys car 5 cwt 4 × 4. **3** Ford 15 cwt 4 × 2 (WOT2). **4** Morris 15 cwt 4 × 2 (CS8).

13 Ambulance markings
These conformed to the ambulance markings employed by all nations, basically a red cross on a white background, painted on each of the rear doors, on each side of the body, on the body roof, and sometimes on cab or bonnet upper surface. The size of the crosses and their square fields on the upper surfaces was determined only by the area available, the markings covering the entire width, but on the rear doors and body sides the crosses were on circular fields of only 18 in (45 cm) diameter. In Burma and the Far East many ambulances had most of the white field painted out, leaving just a white edging to the red cross, allegedly because the Japanese did not always respect the emblems.

14 Other markings
Convoy markings: In order to assist in identifying vehicles belonging to a particular convoy, all vehicles in that convoy were sometimes marked with a convoy number which was applied to the front of the vehicles with chalk. First and last vehicles in the convoy flew blue and green flags respectively. Vehicles being issued to formations and/or units could, whilst in convoy to their destination, be identified by a 10 in (25.4 cm) metal disc, painted royal blue and with a 2 in (5.1 cm) white diagonal, fixed to front and rear of the vehicles. The disc was employed at the discretion of the officer commanding the issuing depot.

To assist in night driving in convoy without lights, all softskins with rear axles visible, and fitted with a lamp to illuminate the rear axle, were to have the rear axle cover plate painted white, creating a circular patch on which could be painted in black the unit's serial number.

Gas detector patches: Prior to October 1943 a patch of gas-sensitive paint, a yellow-khaki in colour, and approximately 18 in (45 cm) square, was sprayed on the front hull of AFVs and on the back of head lamps on other vehicles. After October 1943 it appeared on the bonnet directly in front of the windscreen on softskins, but was no longer applied to AFVs. It was anticipated that gas would be used during World War 2 and, although it was not, these patches were still to be seen on softskins in Europe in 1944.

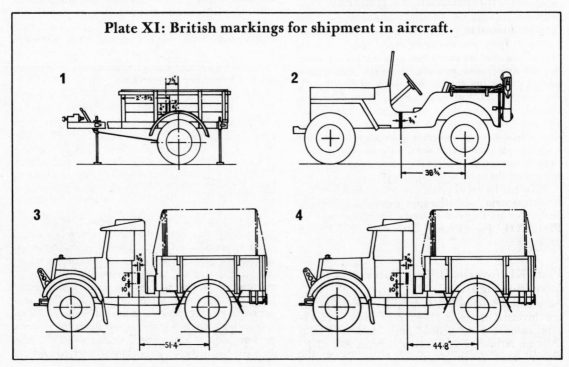

Plate XI: British markings for shipment in aircraft.

Left-hand drive: Vehicles with a left-hand drive and not fitted with trafficators had CAUTION/LEFT HAND DRIVE/NO SIGNALS painted on the rear in 2 in (5.1 cm) high white lettering. Vehicles with trafficators did not carry the NO SIGNALS part of the legend.

Requisitioned vehicles: Civilian vehicles requisitioned in emergencies were to display on the near-side front mudguard and near-side of the tailboard, a label bearing the letters EL. As soon as practicable this was to be replaced by the letters WD painted in 6 in (15.2 cm) high white letters. The WD sign was also applied as a temporary marking to new WD vehicles issued to formations and/or units during an emergency, and lacking their full markings.

Speed limit: The maximum permissible speed was stencilled in red paint on the tailboard, rear panel or equivalent position of all softskins, with the exception of motor cycles and bomb disposal units. Beneath the speed limit figures was printed MPH. The figures were 4 in (10.2 cm) high, letters 2 in (5.1 cm) high, the width of each part of each figure and letter being ½ in (13 mm) and ¼ in (6.5 mm) respectively.

Free Forces

1 National identification marks

Vehicles belonging to units of some foreign forces stationed in Britain, later part of the Allied forces in Italy and north-west Europe, carried a white oval disc on the front, sometimes repeated on the rear, and bearing in black a letter or letters indicating the country of origin, thus PL for Poland, NL for Netherlands, N for Norway. (According to the 1943 regulations the Norwegian forces used a grey oval). Sometimes this emblem was painted directly on to the vehicles. Belgian forces used a small rectangle in their national colours (black/yellow/red) preceding the vehicle serial number.

All other forms of vehicle marking followed the British system, with the exceptions listed below. Examples of formation signs are illustrated in **Plate XII**. Free French forces are dealt with under 'France'.

Plate XII (overleaf): Free Forces formation signs.

1 1st Indep Belgian Bde Grp: yellow lion's head, red inverted triangle. 1943 regs give 'a circle with colours red, yellow and black' for the 'Belgian Army'. **2** 2nd Indep Belgian Bde Grp: yellow lion, green shamrock, red Y. **3** 4th Belgian Inf Bde: yellow grenade, green shamrock, and at top right a small triangle divided into blue and red segments. **4** 5th Belgian Inf Bde: dark green shield, thin yellow inner border, and two chevrons conjoined at horn centre, light green shamrock. **5** 6th Belgian Inf Bde: yellow lion, scarlet diamond of 1st Corps, red/dark blue/red horizontal diamond of 1st Canadian Army, green shamrock. **6** Belgian Forces of the Interior, 1944: yellow lion. **7** 12th Belgian Coy Transport Corps, GT: green shield. **8** 13th Belgian Coy, Trpt Corps, GT: red shield, leopard's head in proper colours. **9** 14th Belgian Coy, Trpt Corps, GT. **10** 15th Belgian Coy, Trpt Corps, GT: red cockerel on yellow disc. **11** 16th Belgian Coy, Trpt Corps, GT: green field and lettering, the two discs at each side of the motto are divided vertically black/yellow/red. **12** Brazilian Expeditionary Force: khaki shield. **13** Czech Indep Armoured Bde Grp: blue shield, red cross, red over blue shield on lion's breast. On vehicles the sign was often simplified to a white lion with the arms of Czechoslovakia on its breast surrounded by a white shield outline, the vehicle colour showing between. **14** Greek Bde Grp: as illustrated on the Wall of Honour, Tobruk, and painted in 1943. **15** 1st Greek Indep Bde, blue field, according to Cole. 2nd Greek Indep Bde also had the head of Minerva but on a blue, diamond-shaped field. 3rd Greek Mountain Bde had the same head but on a square blue field. **16** Cremona Grp (Italian div serving with Allies in Italy): green/white/red with bright blue tower. **17** Frimili Grp: bright blue ear of wheat on same field. **18** Folgore Grp: bright blue arrow on same field. The Piceno Grp used a Roman arch, the Legnano Grp a statue, both in bright blue on a field of the national colours. **19** Jewish Bde Grp: yellow star on light blue/white/light blue field. **20** Royal Netherlands Bde (Princess Irene's): yellow lion. Often used without the background. **21** 1st Netherlands Div: scarlet shield, green wreath, yellow sword hilt. **22** 1st Inf Bde, Royal Netherlands Indonesia Army: yellow bugle, green leaves, dark red 1, on red shield. **23** 2nd Inf Bde RNIA: yellow wings and blade, red shield. **24** Zeeland Bn RNIA: three blue waves. **25** Armoured units, RNIA: red/yellow shield. **26** Armoured units RNIA: variant, red/yellow shield. **27** Royal Yugoslav Forces: royal blue shield. **28** and **29** Vehicle serial number plates, Netherlands East Indies.

7 Tactical markings

Dutch armoured units of the East Indian

Plate XII: Free Forces formation signs.

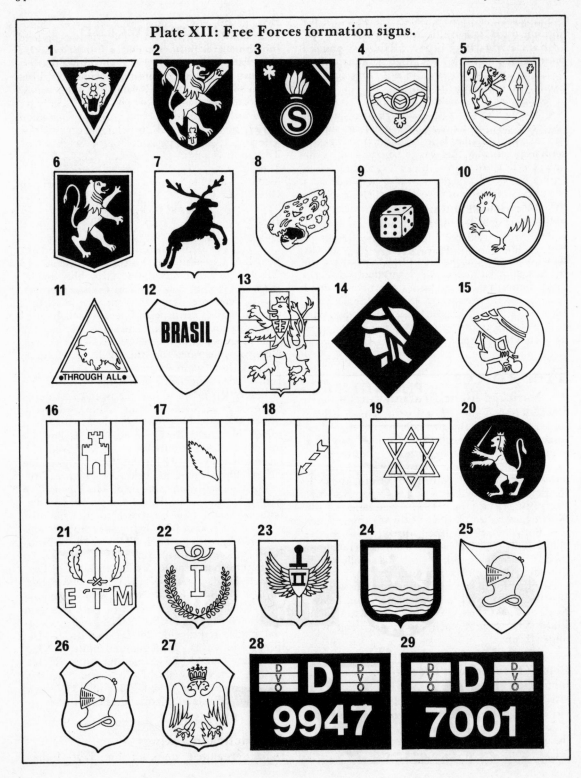

Colonial Army used white, single-digit tactical numbers on their AFVs' turrets in 1940.

Armoured cars of the Singapore Volunteer Force used a white outline of a pennant on their turret sides, with a single-digit tactical number inside. The numbers were repeated on the fronts of the cars.

Yugoslav AFVs had their own system of tactical markings, which seem to have consisted of a number of letters and numerals, for example RRM131. Slogans were also painted on AFV turrets.

10 Vehicle serial numbers

Armoured vehicles of the Netherlands East Indies Army used rectangular licence plates of the type illustrated in **Plate XII Fig 28** (Vickers-Armstrong armoured tracked tractor) and **Fig 29** (Alvis Straussler armoured car). The plates were black with white numbers and letter D. The rectangles on each side of the D appear to have been painted in three colours, probably the national colours of red/white/blue. The D and O on these bands were in white, the V in a colour, probably red.

The Commonwealth

In general the armies of the various countries within the Commonwealth employed the British systems of vehicle markings. Therefore, the various headings below list only variations from the norm.

Africa
4 Formation signs

Examples are illustrated in **Plate XIII**. War Office letters also assigned the following signs: Gambia units, native canoe under sail; Gold Coast units, elephant and palm tree; Nigerian units, crown bird; Sierra Leone units, lion and palm tree. The Kenya Armoured Car Regt had a leopard standing on a green ground painted on the hull sides of its cars.

Plate XIII (below): African formation signs.

1 1st S. African Div: yellow over green. **2** 1st S. African Div: variant used later in war, yellow over green. **3** 2nd S. African Div: yellow over green. **4** 3rd S. African Div: yellow over green. **5**

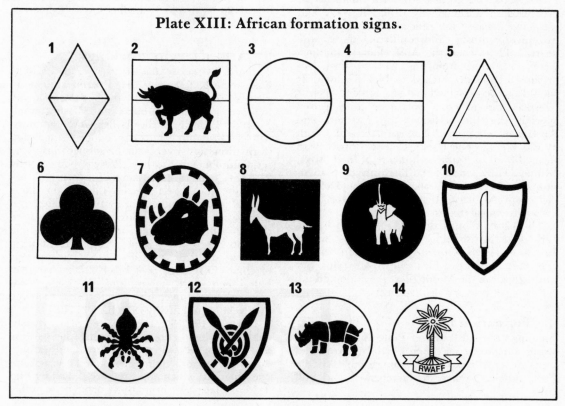

Plate XIII: African formation signs.

6th S. African Div: yellow with green border. **6** 11th African Div. **7** 11th East African Div: red oval. Also shown with continuous black border. An earlier variant had a brown rhino's head on buff oval. **8** 12th African Div. **9** 22nd East African Bde. **10** 28th East African Bde: red shield. **11** 81st West African Div. **12** 82nd West African Div: yellow shield. **13** East African Expeditionary Force. **14** West African Expeditionary Force (Royal West African Frontier Force): yellow, outlined black, on green field.

10   Vehicle serial numbers
Armoured cars built for the South African Union Defence Force had their own run of vehicle serial numbers, which had a U prefix.

Australia
The Australian Army, although using basically the same system of markings as the British, hardly ever carried on its vehicles the same markings as those current in the British Army. Firstly, this was because the Australians were organised in a completely different way, and secondly, because the official regulations were extremely confusing and conflicting during the years 1942-3, when the Australian formations were sent home from the Middle East, re-organised, and despatched to New Guinea. It should also be explained that any force to be sent overseas had to be a volunteer force raised specially for the occasion (the 1st and 2nd Australian Imperial Forces—AIF—of both World Wars) while Home Defence forces were formed from part-time volunteers of the Citizen Military Force, the CMF. The only permanent military forces, PMF, allowed by the Defence Act were Artillery, Instructional Corps, and certain technical troops.

The 18th Infantry Bde (AIF) serving in the UK used British vehicles with the standard British markings. Other AIF formations hardly ever bore markings whilst still in Australia, but once landed in the Middle East they adopted the full range of British style markings.

4   Formation signs
Examples are illustrated in **Plate XIV**. A large white kangaroo was often used by armoured units on captured Italian tanks in the Middle East, usually painted on turret sides and hull sides.

Plate XIV (opposite): Australian and Canadian formation signs (Figs 1-20 Australian).
1 Australian Expeditionary Force, Middle East. **2** 1st Armoured Div. **3** 2nd Armoured Div. **4** 3rd Armoured Div: a variant had a boomerang below the horse. **5** 3rd Tank Bde: a variant had the horse's head without armour. **6** 4th Armoured Bde Grp. **7** 1st Motor Div, originally 1st Cav Div, re-organised March 1942 as motorised, re-organised November 1942 as 3rd Armoured Div, when it adopted the sign shown earlier. **8** 1st Inf Div: also an unofficial variant with aboriginal in kneeling position. **9** 2nd Inf Div. **10** 3rd Inf Div. **11** 4th Inf Div. **12** 5th Inf Div. **13** 6th Inf Div: also used British 6th Div's red star sign for a while in Syria, 1941. **14** 7th Inf Div: a variant adopted in 1943 when the division was allotted an airborne role had the kookaburra in flight but wearing heavy boots because the div was only ever used in an Infantry role. **15** 8th Inf Div. **16** 9th Inf Div; 10th Inf Div used a white snake about to strike, over a boomerang, all on a black square. The 10th existed for only a brief period in 1942. **17** 11th Inf Div. **18** 12th Inf Div. **19** 34th Inf Bde. **20** Tasmanian Defence Force. For **21-28** see text on Canadian forces' formation signs.

6   Arm of service markings
The arm of service flashes used in the Middle East theatre followed the British system in general, but see **Table 9**, which sets out in full the precise serial numbers and flashes used. From 1942 onwards the flashes were combined with the formation signs to produce a single sign (formation sign over arm of service flash and serial number) measuring 9½ by 8½ in (24.1 by 21.6 cm), 6 in (15.2 cm) square for Jeeps.

In the south-west Pacific theatre the same general number and colour systems applied, but there were some variations in the flashes from time to time, especially in 1942. The main variations were: Arty went from red over blue to red/blue divided vertically, then back to the original; Ordnance was black, then red over blue, then black again; and Workshops was black, then red over blue, then black, then red over yellow, and finally went back to black.

During 1942-3 there were also various conflicting instructions concerning the position and width of the white bar used to identify troops at corps and higher level. The various combinations which appeared are shown by **Figs 1-15** in **Plate XV**. From these it can be seen that

Plate XIV: Australian and Canadian formation signs (Figs 1-20 Australian).

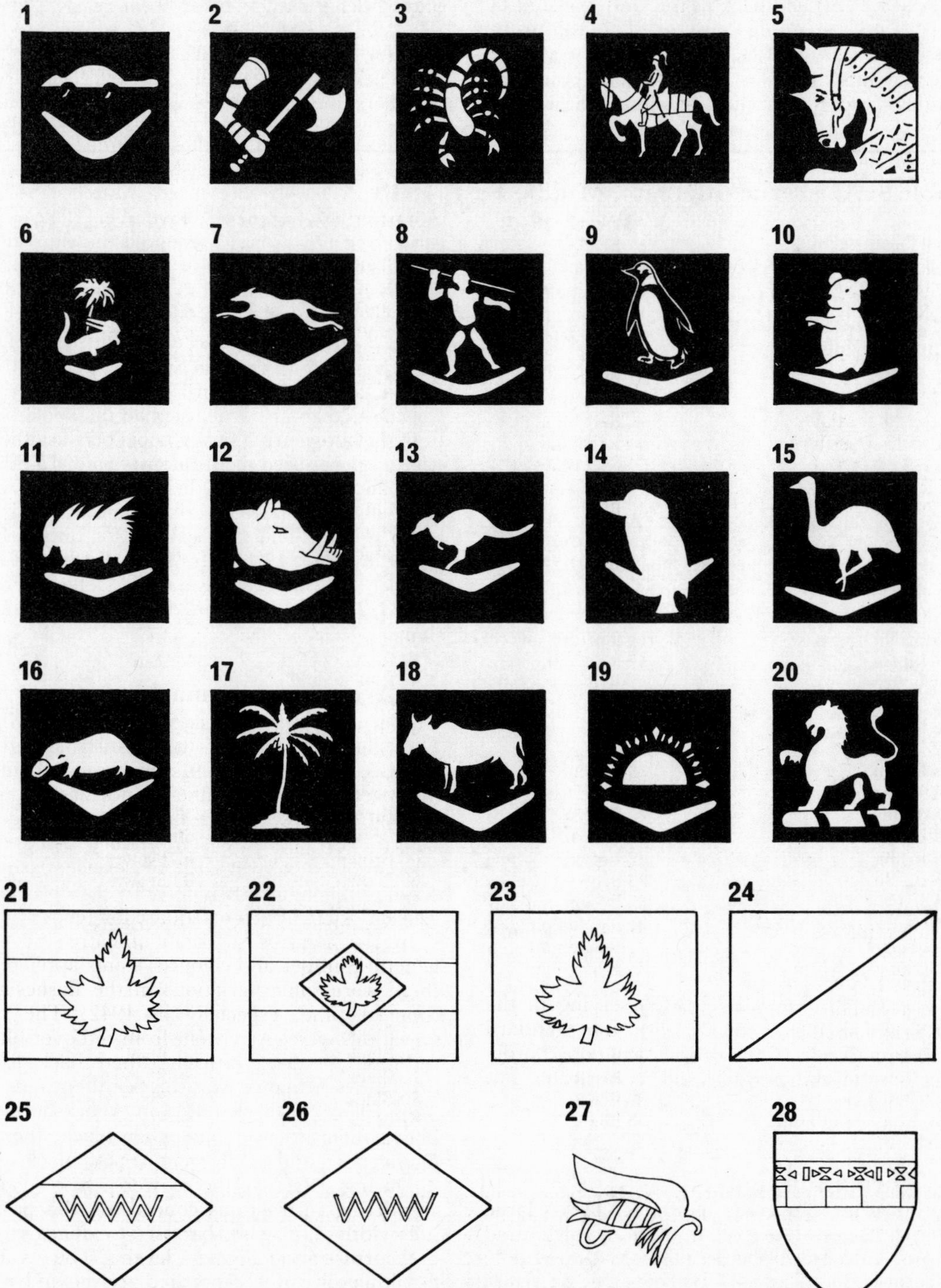

1

2

3

4

5

6

7

8

9

10

11

12

13

14

15

16

17

18

19

20

21

22

23

24

25

26

27

28

the white bars fluctuated between top and bottom of the sign, and also changed from 1 in (25 mm) to 2 in (5.1 cm) and back again, only the L of C units' signs remaining constant. This confusion was ended early in 1943 when the whole system of serial numbers was revised, and groups of numbers were allocated to divs, corps and armies. These numbers were revised again in late 1943. The final allocation was as follows: 100 and under for divs, 100-200 for corps, 200-300 for Armies, 300-600 for L of C units, and 600-999 for Land HQ units. Provided formation signs were used in conjunction with these serial numbers, the white bars previously used by corps

Table 9: AIF serial numbers, Middle East, 1940-2.

Unit	AIF early 1940[1]	9 Div February 1941	9 Div January 1942
HQ 9 Div	1 Black	40 Black	50 Black
Intell Section	1 Black	40 Black	
HQ RAA 9 Div	1 Red/blue	40 Red/blue	82 Red/blue
HQ RAE 9 Div	1 Blue	40 Blue	63 Blue
HQ AASC 9 Div	1 Red/green	40 Red/green	67 Red/green
9 Div Employ Pl	1 Black	40 Black[2]	66 Black
9 Div Cav	2 Black	41 Black	82 Green/blue
2/8 Field Regt RAA	3 Red/blue	42 Red/blue	71 Red/blue
2/7 Field Regt RAA	4 Red/blue	43 Red/blue	88 Red/blue
2/12 Field Regt RAA	5 Red/blue	44 Red/blue	53 Red/blue
3 A/T Regt	6 Red/blue	46 Red/blue	96 Red/blue
24 Field Park Coy RAE	7 Blue	48 Blue	59 Blue
2/3 Field Coy RAA	8 Blue	49 Blue	78 Blue
2/7 Field Coy RAE	9 Blue	50 Blue	70 Blue
2/13 Field Coy RAE	10 Blue	51 Blue	57 Blue
9 Div Signals	11 Black	52 Black[3]	79 White/blue
HQ 20 Bde	12 Red	81 Red	65 Red
2/13 Inf Bn	13 Red	55 Red	91 Red
2/15 Inf Bn	14 Red	56 Red	80 Red
2/17 Inf Bn	15 Red	57 Red	52 Red
20 A/T Coy	33 Red	54 Red	
HQ 24 Bde	16 Green	87 Green	72 Green
2/28 Inf Bn	17 Green	60 Green	84 Green
2/32 Inf Bn	18 Green	61 Green	75 Green
2/43 Inf Bn	19 Green	62 Green	92 Green
24 A/T Coy	34 Green	59 Green	
HQ 26 Bde	20 Brown	94 Brown	58 Brown
2/23 Inf Bn	21 Brown	67 Brown	60 Brown
2/24 Inf Bn	22 Brown	68 Brown	62 Brown
2/48 Inf Bn	23 Brown	69 Brown	89 Brown
26 A/T Coy	35 Brown	64 Brown	
9 Div Ammo Coy AASC	24 Red/green	70 Red/green	69 Red/green
9 Div Petrol Coy	25 Red/green	71 Red/green	74 Red/green
9 Div Supply Column	26 Red/green	72 Red/green	95 Red/green
2/3 Field Ambul	27 Black	75 Black	99 Black
2/8 Field Ambul	28 Black	76 Black	54 Black
2/11 Field Ambul	29 Black	77 Black	86 Black
2/4 Hygiene Sec	30 Black	78 Black	61 Black
9 Div Provost Coy	31 Black	79 Black	68 Black
9 Div Postal Coy	32 Black	80 Black	97 Blue
9 Div Mobile Bath unit	56 Black	67 Black	64 Black
2/2 MG Bn			51 Red[4]
4 LAA Regt[5]			55 Red/blue[6]

1 Provisional numbers, not used by 9th Div, but probably by 6th Div when first in Middle East in 1940. **2** Serial numbers for December 1941, 9th Div, do not include the Employment Platoon. **3** Serial numbers for December 1941, 9th Div, give Signals flash as white over blue, otherwise as February listing. **4** MG Bns were normally Corps Troops. **5** Added to 9th Div list in August-September 1942. LAA Bttys were seldom part of Australian divs, but were usually Corps Troops. **6** Had been red over blue flash, not red/blue diagonal, previous to January 1942 listing.

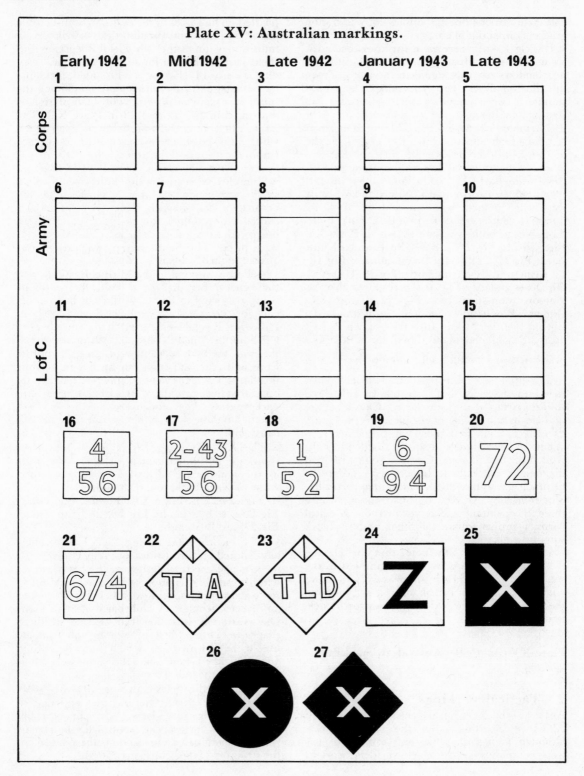

Plate XV: Australian markings.

and Army troops became unnecessary and they gradually went out of use.

During 1944-5 there were two more issues of Vehicle Markings Instructions and the unit serial numbers system was completely revised. From this time on all standard type units were given a standard serial number, for example, all standard Inf bns used the serial number 56, Arty 94, Armour 52, AASC 91. This number, 3 in (7.6 cm) high and in white, was placed on the bottom half of the unit's plate, and above it was painted the numerical designation of the unit. A small white bar, 6½ by 1½ in (16.5 by 3.8 cm) separated the two numbers. Non-standard units were each issued with an individual serial number which stood 6 in (15.2 cm) high. Examples of both types are shown in **Plate XV Figs 16-21: Fig 16**, 4th Inf Bn (standard unit sign); **Fig 17**, 2/43rd Inf Bn (standard); **Fig 18**, 1st Armoured Regt (standard); **Fig 19**, HQ Arty 6th Div (standard); **Fig 20**, Torres Strait Provost Platoon (non-standard); **Fig 21**, Land HQ Cipher Production Section (non-standard). Linked bns, ie, Militia Infantry bns which had been amalgamated, showed both bn numbers to preserve their identities, for example $\frac{37 - 52}{56}$

The same sets of instructions also laid down new arm of service flashes as follows: Inf, a red square; Armour, a green square; Cav, a square divided in half, green over blue; Arty, a square divided in half, red over blue; Engineers, a yellow square; Signals, a square divided in half, white over blue; Service Corps, a square divided diagonally, top right to bottom left, red/green; Ordnance, a square divided into three vertically, blue/red/blue; AEME, a square divided into three horizontally, blue/yellow/red; Medical corps, a brown square; all other units, a black square.

It is interesting to note that, while the Australian Army was by now committed to the south-west Pacific theatre and was working more with US forces than British ones, it still followed the principles of the British system for vehicle markings.

Plate XV (page 39): Australian markings.
See text.

7 Tactical markings

As far as is known tactical signs were not used on AFVs in Australia until the end of 1941, although names on tanks and armoured cars were commonly used for vehicle identification, painted on hull sides to the rear of the unit colour patch and an abbreviated title. However, a militia arty unit, the 9th Field Bde (later 9th Field Regt) did use a tie-on type of tactical sign during early 1941 and it is reasonable to assume that other militia arty units were employing the same or a similar system. The tactical sign is illustrated in **Fig 22** and **23** in **Plate XV**. The larger tilted square was probably red, the letters white, and the smaller square in the top corner was in the colours of the unit patch. The sign was tied to the radiator. This system of positioning was employed because militia units owned only a small proportion of their vehicles, mainly because of lack of space at their depots, and for exercises or summer camps extra vehicles were borrowed from other units or civilian vehicles were hired. The tie-on system was an obvious answer to this problem.

AIF units serving in the Middle East followed the general British system, but, their armour being restricted to Div Cav, did not have much call for geometrical symbols during 1941-2. However, B vehicles did carry letter, number, or letter/number tactical signs on cab doors, sometimes on the body sides instead, and also on the front and rear, although not always in all four positions. The signs were usually painted directly on the vehicles, with white circular or square backgrounds. The official regulations for 1943 stated that these signs should appear only on both cab doors.

The Arty Training Direction of July 1943 shows the permitted tactical signs for arty units as the appropriate tactical letter applied to a white or black background. Examples are shown in **Figs 24-27** in **Plate XV: Fig 24**, regt cmdr; **Fig 25**, 1st Btty cmdr; **Fig 26**, 2nd Btty cmdr; **Fig 27**, 3rd Btty cmdr.

AFV tactical signs during 1942-3 were officially painted on turret sides and rear and were of the same geometrical designs as the British ones, with the single exception of the armoured bde's recce sqdn (1944-5 south-west Pacific) which had an inverted triangle in white for its tactical sign. One variation was that the centres of these shapes were often filled in, creating solid shapes, unlike the British ones, which were in outline only. On Lee/Grant tanks the signs were often repeated on the hull sides.

In the Pacific theatre during 1944-5, AFVs carried their tactical signs on sides and rear of turret, hull sides and glacis. Arty units officially carried their signs on the front of the bonnet or radiator, both cab doors, and on the rear where the structure of the vehicle permitted.

Engineer units also employed tactical signs during the last two years of the war, those of 1945 differing from the ones used in 1944.

Canada

4 Formation signs

Examples are given in **Plate XIV Figs 21-28**; in all cases the maple leaf was yellow.

Fig 21, 1st Army, red/black/red. **Fig 22**, 1st Corps, red/white/red, and red diamond. Also used without the rectangular field. **Fig 22**, 2nd Corps, red/white/red with blue diamond. Also used without the rectangular field. **Fig 23**, 1st Inf Div, red. **Fig 23**, 2nd Inf Div, royal blue, blue letter C in centre of maple leaf. **Fig 23**, 3rd Inf Div, French grey. **Fig 23**, 4th Armoured Div, green. **Fig 23**, 5th Armoured Div, maroon. **Fig 24**, 6th Inf Div, red over blue. **Fig 24**, 7th Inf Div, French grey over dark green. **Fig 24**, 8th Inf Div, maroon over light green. (6th, 7th and 8th Divs were Home Defence units.) **Fig 21**, 1st Armoured Bde, black/red/black. **Fig 21**, 2nd Armoured Bde, black/blue/black. (The rectangular field for these two signs measured 7 by 5½ inches (17.8 by 14 cm).) **Fig 25**, 1st AGRA, red/blue/red, red zigzag on blue. (1st Corps RCA used a similar sign but blue/red/blue with blue zigzag on red.) **Fig 26**, 2nd AGRA, dark blue with red zigzag. **Fig 27**, 64th Coy Service Corps (Army Transport), red with three white bars. **Fig 28**, 85th Coy Service Corps (Bridge), white with red bridge. **Fig 28**, 86th Coy Service Corps (Bridge), white with black bridge.

All these signs were sometimes used without the yellow maple leaf. The diamonds usually shown for 1st and 2nd Armoured Bdes were uniform patches only. The 1943 regulations list the formation sign of the Newfoundland Regts RA as a caribou head in yellow on a red field.

6 Arm of service markings

These followed the same pattern as in the British Army: full serial numbers for formations in north-west Europe are given in **Tables 10** and **11**.

7 Tactical markings

As for the British Army, except that in some armoured units A Sqdns used the triangle inverted.

8 Call signs

Canadian forces in England in 1943 used a single letter prefix to what appear to have been call signs. The following letter-number combinations have been seen: C32, C33, H-11, H-19, Z19.

Table 11: Formation attached 5th Canadian Armoured Div.*

Unit	Serial	Flash
HQ 12 Cdn Inf Bde	81	Red
12 Cdn Inf Bde Ground Defence Pl	81	Red
12 Cdn Independent MG Coy	81	Red
4 Cdn PLDG Bn	55	Red
1 Cdn LAA Bn	56	Red
Westminster Regt (Motorised)	54	Red

*This formation existed for the period July 1944 to March 1945 only.

Table 10: Serial numbers and flashes of the 1st Canadian Armoured Bde (Independent).

Unit	Serial	Flash
Bde HQ	172	Blue
11th Armoured Regt	173	Blue
12th Armoured Regt	174	Blue
14th Armoured Regt	175	Blue
Bde Signals	172	White/blue
1st Cdn Armoured Bde Coy (83 Coy)	176	Red/green
2nd Light Field Ambulance	169	Black
1st Cdn Armoured Bde Ordnance Fd Park	656	Blue/red/blue
1st Cdn Armoured Bde Workshop	99	Blue/yellow/red
1st Cdn Tank Troops Workshop	5393	Blue/yellow/red
59 Cdn LAD (11th Armoured Regt)	173	Blue/yellow/red
60 Cdn LAD (12th Armoured Regt)	174	Blue/yellow/red
61 Cdn LAD (14th Armoured Regt)	175	Blue/yellow/red
3rd Cdn Provost Section	5075	Black

Note: Canadian armoured and Inf Divs used the same serial numbers and flashes as their British counterparts in 1944-5.

Most of these markings were in solid white, but some tactical numbers on Canadian AFVs were in red edged white.

10 Vehicle serial numbers

Prefixes were as for the British Army, but usually preceded in turn by the letter C, thus CT for tanks, CL for lorries, etc. The Canadian manufactured Rams had the following serial numbers: Mark I, CT39781-397830; Mark IIa, CT397831-39980; Mark IIb, CT39981-40100; Mark IIc, CT40101-40437; Mark IId, 40438-40937 and CT159402-159501; Mark IIe, CT159502-160193.

India

4 Formation signs

Examples are illustrated in **Plates XVI** and **XVII**.

6 Arm of service markings

These followed the British system in general, but with the following known exceptions: prior to mid-1942 the three regts of 31st Armoured Div in Persia and Syria used the serial numbers 142, 143, 144. Thereafter they conformed to the serial numbers used by British forces in the Middle East. In 1944 the three regts of 44th Armoured Div in India used the serial numbers 118, 119, 120 on a two-colour flash: in 1945 they used the standard British serial numbers but still on the two-colour flash.

10 Vehicle serial numbers

Indian forces used a six or seven figure serial number, preceded by a WD arrow. The first two figures of the numbers were much smaller than the remainder, and were sometimes omitted altogether. The numbers and WD arrow were usually painted in white on a rectangular black background, but black on white was sometimes used, depending on the vehicle colour.

Plate XVI (opposite) Indian formation signs.

1 31st Armoured Div: green field. **2** 32nd Armoured Div: grey on red. **3** 43rd Armoured Div: red horns, hooves and eyes. 44th Armoured Div, formed from 32nd and 43rd Armoured Divs in January 1943, had the same sign but with the motto LARO AUR LARTE RAHO round the edge of the field above the buffalo. **4** 2nd Armoured Bde: scarlet field. **5** 3rd Armoured

Bde: red shield with narrow white inner border, on yellow square. **6** 50th Tank Bde. **7** 251st Tank Bde: red field. **8** 254th Tank Bde: red inverted triangle and three drops of blood below it. **9** 255th Tank Bde: red eyes, hooves and horns, blue field. **10** 2nd Inf Div: yellow hornet. **11** 3rd Inf Div: yellow dragon, blue field. **12** 4th Inf Div: red eagle. **13** 5th Inf Div: red disc. **14** 6th Inf Div: yellow tiger's head. **15** 7th Inf Div: yellow arrow: also used on black circular field. **16** 8th Inf Div: yellow, according to 1943 regs. Cole gives red field. **17** 9th Inf Div: royal blue star. **18** 10th Inf Div: pink bar over blue one. **19** 11th Inf Div. **20** 12th Inf Div: yellow with lion outlined in blue. **21** 14th Inf Div. **22** 17th Inf Div: khaki field. In 1942 the division used a dark blue square as a sign. **23** 19th Inf Div: yellow on red field. **24** 20th Inf Div. **25** 21st Inf Div: red horns, blue field. **26** 23rd Inf Div: red cockerel on yellow field. **27** 25th Inf Div: green field. **28** 26th Inf Div: yellow tiger, blue triangle. **29** 39th Inf Div: dark green field. **30** 44th Airborne Div: maroon field, pale blue INDIA, Bellerophon and Pegasus.

Plate XVII (page 44): Indian and New Zealand formation signs.

1 3rd Motor Bde: red horseshoe. **2** 38th Inf Bde: red head, neck and legs, blue body. **3** 43rd Lorried Inf Bde: dark green field. **4** 52nd Inf Bde: green fish. **5** 60th Inf Bde: red and white lance pennants. **6** 72nd Inf Bde: red circle. **7** 116th Inf Bde: yellow, royal blue field, yellow border. Also seen as black axe and border on khaki field. **8** 150th Inf Bde: yellow bayonet. **9** 155th Inf Bde: yellow. **10** 268th Inf Bde: red horns, blue field. **11** Lushai Bde: red field. **New Zealand signs: 12** New Zealand Expeditionary Force: red stars. 1943 regs give a similar sign for non-div troops, but make no mention of white edging round the stars. **13** New Zealand Expeditionary Force, as painted on the Wall of Honour at Tobruk in 1943. 1943 regs give this sign, the national emblem, for the 'New Zealand Div'. **14** 1st Inf Div. **15** 2nd Inf Div. **16** 3rd Inf Div. **17** 4th Inf Div. **18** 5th Inf Div. 6th Inf Div had same sign as 3rd Inf Div. **19** New Zealand 4th Armoured Bde.

New Zealand

4 Formation signs

Examples are illustrated in **Plate XVII; Figs 12-19**.

Plate XVI: Indian formation signs.

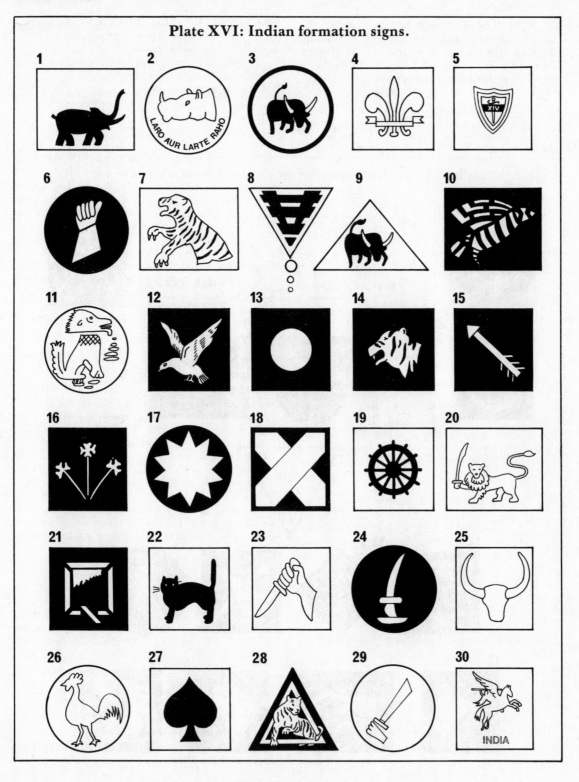

6   Arm of service markings

Flashes and serial numbers were as set out in **Table 12**. The three regts of 4th Armoured Bde, part of 2nd Div in North Africa after El Alamein and in Italy, used the serial numbers 91, 80, 52 in Italy.

7   Tactical markings

Geometrical signs as for British forces, except their use was restricted to the AFVs of the div's 'Cav' unit. Other units used numbers only. Official instructions stipulated:

'Divisional Cavalry will have the signs painted in white on both sides of each vehicle.

'Troop numbers will be painted in white immediately below these signs. Individual AFVs may be named.

'No other unit will have vehicle tactical signs.

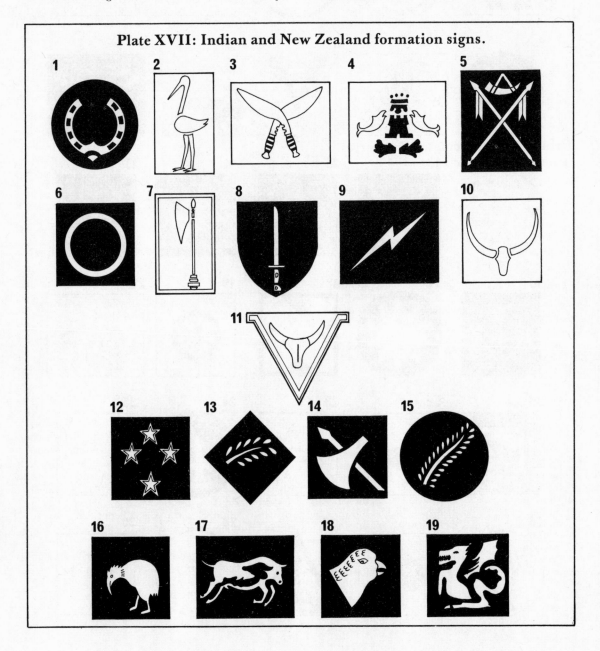

Plate XVII: Indian and New Zealand formation signs.

'All units will number their vehicles under unit arrangements. Vehicle numbers will be painted on both sides of the vehicle.'

14   Other markings

Official instructions state:

'NZASC load-carrying vehicles will in addition display the signs authorised in RASC Training, viz:

'Ammunition vehicles: royal blue rectangle with a white square centre.

'Petrol vehicles: royal blue disc with a white circular centre.

'Supply vehicles: royal blue equilateral triangle with a white circular centre.

'Blanket vehicles: royal blue diamond with a white diamond centre.'

Table 12: New Zealand Div Serial Numbers, Middle East, 1941.

Unit	Early 1941	From October 1941
Div HQ	1 Black	50 Black
Employ Platoon	1 Black	77 Black
Intell Section	1 Black	Not listed
HQ Arty	1 Red/blue	82 Red/blue
HQ Engineers	1 Blue	63 Blue
HQ NZASC	1 Red/green	67 Red/green
Div Cav	2 Black	81 Green/blue
4 Field Regt	3 Red/blue	88 Red/blue
5 Field Regt	4 Red/blue	71 Red/blue
6 Field Regt	5 Red/blue	53 Red/blue
7 A/T Regt	6 Red/blue	96 Red/blue
36 Survey Btty[1]	40 Red/blue	3 Red/blue
5 Field Park Coy	7 Blue	59 Blue
6 Field Coy	8 Blue	78 Blue
7 Field Coy	9 Blue	70 Blue
8 Field Coy	10 Blue	57 Blue
Div Signals	11 Black	79 Blue/white
HQ 4 Inf Bde[2]	12 Red	65 Red
18 Inf Bn	13 Red	91 Red
19 Inf Bn	14 Red	80 Red
20 Inf Bn	15 Red	52 Red
HQ 5 Inf Bde	16 Green	72 Green
21 Inf Bn	17 Green	84 Green
22 Inf Bn	18 Green	75 Green
23 Inf Bn	19 Green	92 Green
HQ 6 Inf Bde	20 Brown	58 Brown
24 Inf Bn	21 Brown	60 Brown
25 Inf Bn	22 Brown	62 Brown
26 Inf Bn	23 Brown	89 Brown
27 (MG) Bn	37 Black	51 Red
28 (Maori) Bn	38 Black	23 Black
Ammo Coy NZASC	24 Red/green	69 Red/green
Petrol Coy	25 Red/green	74 Red/green
Supply Column	26 Red/green	95 Red/green
Reserve MT Coy	39 Red/green	48 Red/green
4 Field Ambulance	27 Black	99 Black
5 Field Ambulance	28 Black	54 Black
6 Field Ambulance	29 Black	86 Black
4 Field Hygiene Sec	30 Black	61 Black
Mobile Bath unit	36 Black	64 Black
Provost Coy	31 Black	68 Black
Postal unit	32 Black	97 Blue
14 LAA Regt[3]		55 Red/blue
Ordnance Workshop[3]		26 Black
Ordnance Field Park[3]		19 Black

1 Listed as 1 Survey Troop in October 1941. **2** Listed as Bde HQ and Defence Platoon in October 1941. **3** Added in October 1941. Survey Troop, 28 Bn, Reserve MT Coy, Ordnance Workshop and Field Park were not in fact allocated new numbers and flashes until November 7 1941.

France

1   National identification marks

All AFVs carried the French tricolour, blue white/red, as a national identification mark. Before the fall of France in 1940 this was about 15 cm deep by 22.5 cm long and was painted on the hull front and rear of most types of tanks, normally preceding the vehicle's serial number, although it might occasionally be placed above or below that number. An exception to this rule was the Char B tank, on which it nearly always appeared below the tank's name on the glacis. Char Bs also frequently had the tricolour repeated on the left side of the turret.

French forces in North Africa continued to use the tricolour as a national identification mark after 1940, but then it was often painted on the hull sides as well, and when these forces were fully equipped with US or British AFVs, the tricolour normally appeared on front, rear and both sides of the hull. From 1943 the tricolour was usually surrounded by a narrow white edge, as shown in **Fig 1** in **Plate XVIII**.

Most AFVs pre-1940 also carried tricolour roundels, measuring 30 cm in diameter on turrets, up to 50 cm in diameter on hulls. There were sometimes as many as five such roundels on a tank; on hull rear and both sides, and on both the rearmost angles of the turret sides. Occasionally the roundels had a narrow edging of white. Char Bs did not as a general rule carry these roundels, but on May 19 1940 some Char Bs of 46th Bn de Chars de Combat were fired on by other French tanks, and thereafter the 46th and 41st Bns, and the 352nd Independent Coy, had roundels on their tanks. The roundel was not used after the fall of France by those forces escaping to Britain, nor in North Africa after 1943, when a link up between the Army in Africa

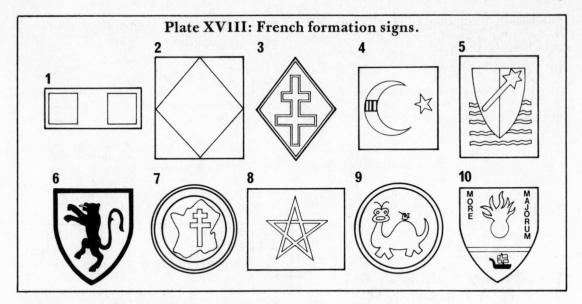

Plate XVIII: French formation signs.

and Free French units enabled the organisation of a new French Army to begin.

From late 1943 some of these new formations used a new symbol in place of the tricolour, see **Fig 2** in **Plate XVIII**: top left and bottom right red, other two corners blue, remainder white. This symbol sometimes had FRANCE ABORD stencilled across it in two lines in black. The Forces Françaises de L'Intérieur—the official combination of all French Resistance movements—used either the letters FFI or a large cross of Lorraine in white on any captured or commandeered vehicles they employed. **Plate XVIII Fig 3** shows the emblem used by the Free French forces fighting alongside the Allies: a red cross of Lorraine, edged white, on a blue diamond, edged red.

2 Aerial recognition symbols

Prior to the fall of France the national identification roundel occasionally appeared on turret tops as an aerial recognition sign, but no other symbols were used for this purpose; presumably it was thought the profusion of roundels gave sufficient indication of nationality. During 1944-5 some AFVs used the national identification symbol illustrated by **Fig 2 Plate XVIII** on their turret tops, but most used the Allied white star as employed by US and British forces in north-west Europe.

3 Rank, signal and other flags

No information, except some regimental pennants, and less frequently standards, were

flown from tank aerials or on car wings both in North Africa and Europe.

4 Formation signs

Units did not carry formation signs prior to the fall of France, but the Free French units organised in Britain and later serving in Italy and north-west Europe adopted the British practice of painting such signs on their vehicles: location was as for British vehicles. These signs remained in use when the French Army was reborn with its own divs and corps. Some examples of the signs are illustrated in **Plate XVIII; Figs 4-10.**

Plate XVIII (above): French formation signs.

Figs 1-3 are national identification symbols, see text. **4** 1st Army in Algeria and Tunisia 1943: green field, small tricolour on crescent. Reconstruction. **5** 1st Army 1944-5: yellow mace on red/green shield, dark blue field with light blue wavy lines. **6** 1st Div 1944-5: lion rampant with red eyes, tongue and claws on yellow shield. **7** 2nd Armoured Div 1944-5: red cross on white outline of France, on blue field surrounded by white then blue edging. **8** 4th Moroccan Div 1943-5: green outline of star, red field. **9** 2nd Indep Bde 1942: red animal, blue edging to field. **10** 13th Demi-Bde de Légion Etrangère: red flaming grenade, gold lettering, blue bar above ship on blue sea with blue cross on sail.

5 Regimental insignia

Unit signs were occasionally painted on vehicles

in the 1939-40 period, particularly on the lorries of the transport companies. These signs were usually a simplified version of the unit badges. The practice was continued by many units in North Africa and the UK after the fall of France. On AFVs the signs usually appeared on the hull sides, on the cab doors of softskins. Some examples of these signs are illustrated in **Plate XIX**.

Plate XIX (below): French formation signs; regimental.

1 Bn de Marche No 11: red hat and cross on light green shield with blue heading bearing BM in light green. Most infantry units used a similar shield without the man's head, and bearing their own number. **2** Bn de Marche No 1: green cross on yellow triangle. **3** 1st Bn d'Infanterie de

Plate XIX: French formation signs; regimental.

Marine: red cross edged gold, blue anchor, gold rope, date and lettering on blue scroll. **4** 2nd Coy same unit: gold cross on tricolour in form of disc. **5** Regt de Marche du Tchad: red cross on blue/white/red shield. **6** 1st Bn de Fusiliers Marins Commandos: stencilled on unit's cars in 1944, red cross and dagger, white ship and lettering, vehicle paint showing elsewhere. **7** Units rallying in Oubangui: red cross edged white on blue shield. **8** Légion du Cameroun: red cross and gold chevron. **9** Units rallying in Nord-Cameroun: red cross on blue/white/red bend on white shield, red letters and border. **10** 5th Regt Automobile: blue cog, red on white inner discs, white arrow, colour of shield and lettering unknown. **11** 101st Compagnie Automobile, N Africa: colours unknown, probably blue or black cog, white field, blue and red uprights to H. **12** 2nd Compagnie Anti-Chars: red star, cross and lettering. **13** 21st Coy Nord-Africaine: red star, blue disc edged white, white cross on blue disc edged white, both on red disc. **14** Détachment d'Artillerie du C^t de Conchard: pale blue cross, gold crossed gun barrels, FFL in blue/white/gold respectively, on orange shield, overall a green bend bearing in gold VAILLANS RIEN IMPOSSIBLE. **15** Escadron de Spahis Marocains, Sudan-Egypt 1940-1: very pale blue cross on light blue star. **16** Escadron de Spahis Marocains, Egypt 1941: gold star. **17** Escadron Mécanisé Nord-Syrie: red cross and armoured car outline, light blue smaller disc and letters, medium blue larger disc. **18** Col Collet's Circassian Sqdn, Syria 1941: probably black on white, colour of crescent unknown. **19** Génie au Levant: probably white surround, red cross edged white, there should be a white sword blade down centre of anchor, colour of vehicle showing through elsewhere as the field. **20** Unknown unit, 1939-40 period: green over white. **21** Unknown unit, 1939-40: yellow lion, red shield. **22** Unknown unit, 1939-40: red winged wheel. **23** Unknown unit: yellow emblem with white shape of France direct on vehicle colour.

6 Arm of service markings

So far as is known, no symbols were used prior to the fall of France. From 1943 until the end of the war, arm of service was indicated by a letter, painted on a divisional colour on the hull side: A Arty; B Inf; C Armour; F AA; G Engineers; K Transport; M Reinforcement unit; R Recce unit; S Medical unit; T Signals; X Ordnance; X Div HQ and HQ Coy; Y Tank Destroyer unit.

Combat commands were indicated by the first letter of the commander's name: see **Table 13** for examples of these codes in use.

7 Tactical markings

Prior to the fall of France different marking systems were employed by the various types of formation. The Div Légère Mécanique, employing mostly Light tanks (R35s, R40s, FCM36s, and H35s) retained the World War 1 system of playing card symbols. Under this system each coy was identified by a geometrical symbol painted on the turret rear or sides, either solid or in outline only: 1st Coy, a circle 35 cm in diameter; 2nd Coy, a square 30 cm each side; 3rd Coy, an isosceles triangle 45 cm at base, 40 cm high. Each section within the coy had painted on this symbol a playing card suit: 1st Platoon the ace of spades; 2nd the ace of hearts; 3rd the ace of diamonds; and 4th the ace of clubs. In some three-section coys the ace of clubs was allocated to the reserve or replacement platoon. The colour of the playing card symbol also identified the bn within a regt: blue for 1st Bn, red for 2nd.

Table 13: Unit sign 2nd French Armoured Div NW Europe, 1944-5.

Div HQ	X̄			
Combat Commands*	D	R	L	V
501st Regt de Chars de Combat	C̄			
12th Regt de Chasseurs d'Afrique	|C|			
12th Regt de Cuirassiers	|C̄|			
HQ Regt de Marche du Tchad	B			
1st, 2nd, 3rd Bns	B̄	|B|	|B̄|	
HQ 13th Bn du Genie	G			
1st, 2nd, 3rd, 4th, 16th Coys	Ḡ	|G	|G|	Ḡ
HQ Regt Blinde des Fusiliers Marins	Y			
1st, 2nd, 3rd, 4th Troops	Ȳ	Y̶	Y̶	Ȳ
HQ 1st Regt de Marche de Spahis Marocains	R			
1st, 2nd, 3rd Troops	R̄	|R|	|R̄|	
HQ Div Arty	A			
HQ XI Groupe du 64th Regt d'artillerie	Ā			
31st, 32nd, 33rd, Service Btties	|Ā	|Ā	|Ā	|Ā
397, 197, 297, 497 Transport Coys	K	K̄	|K|	|K̄|
HQ 22nd Groupe AA	F			
1st, 2nd, 3rd, 4th sub-units	F̄	|F	|F|	F̲
HQ 13th Medical Bn	S			
1st, 2nd, 3rd Coys	S̄	S̱	S̄	
Reinforcement Unit	M			
97th/84th Coy Signals	|T|			

*Combat Commands adopted the letter of their cmdr's surname:—Dio, Remy, Langlade and Vazabian.

The H35s and H39/40s of the Cav formations used a two number system, the numbers being painted in white and very large on the rearmost angled surfaces of the turret sides. Some examples seen appear to indicate the tank's position within a sqdn: 2-7, 2-9, 3-5, 3-8, 4-0, 4-3, 4-4, 4-5 (all on H39/40s, with one digit appearing on each side of the turret rear), but others are the same number repeated on both sides: 80-80, 95-95 (on H35s), while some H39s have only a single digit number on their turret sides nearest the front.

The Heavy tanks of the Div Cuirassée also used large white numbers on turret sides, but Char B units had their own system of a large white letter painted on the hull sides and repeated on the turret sides. On rare occasions the letter also appeared on the hull rear. These letters were chosen by the bn or coy cmdr and a different letter was allocated to each section of three tanks. Known examples are listed in **Table 15**. However, it would appear that some Char B units used the geometrical coy symbols described for the Light tanks, these symbols being painted on turret rear or sides. The playing card symbols were not used.

The ten Char 2C Super tanks of the 51st Tank Bn also used large numbers, painted in solid white on the hull sides, usually at the front end, or below the front turret. The numbers were 'blocked' with black paint. The only examples seen are 93 and 97, used in conjunction with the names Alsace and Normandie respectively.

Armoured cars seem to have used a single digit number, painted in white on the turret sides, or on angled surfaces towards the top front of the turret.

The French forces fighting in the Middle East under British command adopted the British system of tactical markings, but from 1943 in Italy and 1944 in north-west Europe the French formations used their own system. This consisted of a 10 in (25.3 cm) square painted on the hull sides towards the rear and repeated on the hull front (see **Plate XX, Figs 4** and **5**), the square being yellow for 2nd Armoured Div, green and red for the other two armoured divs. The arm of service letter was painted on this square in white, and vertical and horizontal bars were placed round the letter to indicate sub-units within a regt. The complete set of markings for 2nd Armoured Div is set out in **Table 13**.

Plate XX (overleaf): Markings locations.
Figs 1-3 illustrate location of markings on Char B1: **1** = Letter. **2** = Name. **3** = Three-digit number. **4** = Tricolour. **5** = Roundel. **Figs 4 and 5** illustrate location of markings on Shermans: **1** = Call sign. **2** = Tricolour. **3** = Unit tactical sign. **4** = Call sign. **5** = Name. **6** = Formation sign. **7** = Serial number. **8** = Shipping marks.

8 Call signs
Not in use for the 1939-40 period. From 1943 units fighting in Italy, and from 1944 those fighting in north-west Europe, employed large two-digit numbers either painted on the hull or turret sides in white to indicate a vehicle's position within a sub-unit. See under Britain, section 8.

9 Vehicle names
During the 1939-40 period only the Char B and Char 2C units employed names on their tanks. The only known examples for Char 2 Cs are Alsace and Normandie, painted in white and 'blocked' with black. The Char B system is set out in **Table 14**, and known examples are listed in **Table 15**. On Char Bs the names were painted in white and were about 15 cm high.

Vehicle names were very popular during the 1943-5 period, and appear in large white lettering on the hull sides of many Shermans: provinces, battles and the names of famous French people were used, but no coherent pattern has yet been identified.

10 Vehicle serial numbers
Until the fall of France, French tanks had the following groupings of vehicle serial numbers (based on pictorial evidence alone): 101-470, Char Bs, as listed in **Table 14**. 1100 range, Char D1. 2000-2200 range, Char D2. 30000 range, FCM36, 40600 range, R39/40. 40959 range,

Table 14: Char B vehicle names and serial numbers.

Serial	Name theme	Unit
101-135	Provinces	37th BCC*
201-235	Provinces, colonies, towns	15th BCC
236-270	Frigates and destroyers	8th BCC
271-305	Colonial towns	28th BCC
306-345	Rivers	41st and 49th BCC
346-375	Wines	41st and 49th BCC
376-387	1914-18 victories	41st and 49th BCC
388-410	1914-18 victories	46th and 47th BCC
411-431	French war leaders	46th and 47th BCC
432-470	?	later replacement vehicles (?)

*BCC: Bn de Chars de Combat.

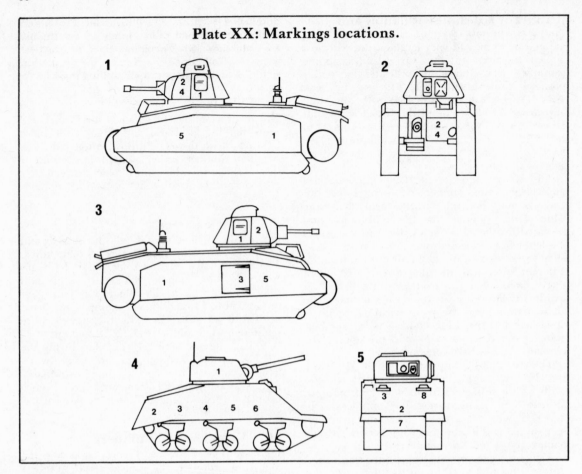

Plate XX: Markings locations.

H39 and possibly H35. 50200-50800, R35. 51000-51600, R35. R39/40 followed after the 51000 range. 80000 range, Renault FT17. 81700 range, AMR Renault 33VM. 91000 range, Renault FT17.

All serial numbers were painted, often stencilled, in white on hull front and rear, most often on the right hand side of each. Char Ds had the number repeated on the hull sides. Char Bs usually had the number repeated on the access door on the right hand side.

Units fighting in the Middle East, Italy and north-west Europe later in the war kept the serial numbers already on those vehicles supplied by the British or US Armies.

11   Bridge classification numbers

No information for the 1939-40 period. As UK and USA numbers later in the war, depending on which country supplied the vehicle.

12   Shipping and rail loading marks

Not applicable pre-1943. As UK and USA systems thereafter, depending which country supplied the vehicle.

13   Ambulance markings

During the 1939-40 period red crosses on small white squares were painted on the body sides, with beneath them the lettering SERVICE/DE/ SANTE, with the section number below that. In the last years of the war the UK-USA markings were used.

14   Other markings

Before the fall of France all towing vehicles carried a small signboard secured vertically on the cab roof. The board was black and bore a white triangle, the base of which stretched across the entire width of the board's bottom edge, while its apex touched the board's upper edge.

Table 15: Examples of names and serials on Char Bs.

Name	Serial	Letter	BCC No
Adour	—	—	37 (Coy cmdr)
Aquitaine	—	—	15 (?)
Auvergne	118	None	8
Arlay	388	—	41
Bourrasque	—	—	8 (?)
Colmar	—	None	15 or 37
Dunkerque	111	U	37
Eclair	268	D	8 (2nd Coy cmdr)
Fantasque	251	None	8
Flandres	128	B	37
Gard	—	S	37 (3rd Coy)
Guepratte	438	T	37 (3rd Coy)
Herault	—	—	37
Madagascar	206	—	15 (2nd Coy)
Malin (later Luneville)	245	—	8
Maréchal Petain	414	—	46
Martinique	—	—	15
Nancy II*	—	X	? (as Vendee II)
Nivernais II	467	U	?
Ourcq	—	—	37
Poitou II	—	3	?
Rapide	—	None	8 (?)
Rhône	—	M	37
Somme	340	—	41 or 49
Temeraine	—	—	8 (?)
Toulon	—	—	15
Tempete	—	—	8 (?)
Villers-Brettoneux	–	—	15
Var	?	S	37 (3rd Coy)
Vendée II	468	X	?
Verdun II	452	4A	?
Yonne	—	—	41 (2nd Coy)

*Indicates second tank (replacement) of this name.

Poland

In 1939 Poland had the sixth largest Army in Europe. I regret that I have no real information on the markings carried on the vehicles of this Army in its brief but heroic struggle against Nazi Germany and the USSR. It would appear that the Army's AFVs rarely carried markings, a single known exception being the 1st Tank Bn, whose 7TP jw Light tanks carried a white or yellow bison, within a circle of the same colour, on their turret sides.

After the fall of Poland a large part of her Army went into captivity in the USSR, but part escaped to France, where it was re-organised under General Sikorski. The 1st and 2nd Armoured Bns were formed in January 1940, the 1st being transferred to the South of France and equipped with World War 1 Renault tanks, the 2nd being sent to Versailles, armed with R40 tanks, and attached to the French 1st Corps. It is presumed the vehicles used by these units bore French style markings.

On the fall of France, part of the Polish forces in that country managed to escape to Britain, where they were re-organised into the 1st (Polish) Armoured Div in January 1942. Later the Independent Parachute Bde was formed. These formations adopted the British style of markings for their vehicles.

When the Allies supplied the USSR with arms, part of the deal was the release of Polish soldiers from captivity. By 1942 many Poles had been released and organised into the 5th and 6th Infantry Divs in Iraq under British command. Later the 2nd Armoured Bde was formed. These formations moved into Egypt in 1943, and in December that year landed in Italy. As more Poles were released by the USSR, so these formations were increased in strength and number to form the 2nd Polish Corps.

One other Polish formation in the Middle East was the Independent Carpathian Bde, organised in French Syria in 1940. After the fall of France this bde crossed into Palestine and served in the North African campaign under British command. It became the 3rd Carpathian Rifle Div in December 1943 and went to Italy with the 2nd Polish Corps. All vehicles used by these formations were of British or US origin and the British markings' systems were applied.

Meanwhile, the Soviets had also organised some Polish units. These were equipped with Soviet vehicles and, so far as can be ascertained, used the Soviet system of markings.

1 National identification marks

As for British forces in the Middle East and north-west Europe, except that Polish units stationed in the UK also carried the letters PL in black on a white oval on the right front and left rear of their vehicles.

In the USSR some tanks manned by Polish crews towards the end of the war had the white Polish eagle painted on the turret sides after the tactical number.

2 Aerial recognition symbols

As British forces in Middle East and north-west Europe.

3 Rank, signal and other flags

Each regt had a distinctive pennant but, according to research at the Polish Institute and Sikorski Museum in London, these pennants were only flown on AFVs for parades, being secured to the A set aerial. Inevitably there are exceptions to the rule, and Eddy Florentine in his book *The Battle of Falaise Gap* describes the Cromwells and Stuarts of the 10th Mounted Rifles (armoured recce regt of 1st Armoured Div) going into action with their emerald green/ white/yellow 'standards' flying. Therefore, the pennants of those units within 1st Armoured Div which were equipped with AFVs have been listed here: see **Plate XXI Figs 17-20** for the various designs:

Fig 17, Div and 10th Armoured Cav Bde HQs, black with orange triangle next to the hoist. **Fig 17**, 3rd Rifles Bde HQ, blue with yellow triangle next to the hoist. **Fig 18**, 1st Armoured Regt, black over orange with red stripe. **Fig 18**, 2nd Armoured Regt, black over orange with white stripe. **Fig 18**, 24th Lancers, white with yellow stripe. **Fig 18**, 10th Drgns, brownish-red over orange with light green stripe. **Fig 19**, Highland Rifle Bn, blue over yellow. **Fig 19**, 8th Rifles Bn, green over blue. **Fig 20**, 9th Flanders Rifle Bn, yellow over blue with blue over yellow stripes. **Fig 20**, 1st Indep HMG Sqdn, yellow over brownish-red with blue over white stripes. **Fig 18**, 10th Mounted Rifles, light green over mustard yellow with white stripe. **Fig 19**, 1st Tank Replacement Sqdn, black over orange.

Many tanks of 2nd Corps in Egypt also carried flags, mostly a small square one with a chequer pattern. Nothing is known about signal flags.

4   Formation signs

As British system: all known signs for Polish forces are illustrated in **Plate XXI**.

From September 1944 HQ Polish forces in the UK adopted a vehicle marking consisting of a combination of the white Polish eagle on red and the red Scottish lion on yellow, the actual design is not known.

Fig 10 (2nd Army Tank Bde) was the pre-war sign of the Polish Armoured Corps. Later this was changed to a black knight's helmet with visor and plume on a yellow square, and when re-organised into the 2nd Armoured Bde in January 1944 the unit adopted the sign of the 2nd Armoured Div.

Plate XXI (opposite): Polish formation signs.

1 1st Polish Corps: in white on all vehicles until September 1943. **2** 1st Armoured Div: orange centre to circle, white outlining round helmet. **3** Indep Para Bde. **4** Indep Carpathian Bde: red shield. **5** 3rd Carpathian Rifle Div: green tree on

white over red field. **6** HQ Polish Army, Middle East, from July 1943: red towers. **7** L of C units, Middle East, from July 1943: white over red field. **8** 2nd Polish Corps, from July 1943: red shield. Before this date used by HQ Polish Forces, Middle East. **9** 2nd Armoured Div. **10** 2nd Army Tank Bde: black, or possibly dark blue, and orange. **11** 14th Armoured Bde: dark yellow field. **12** 16th Armoured Bde: silver and grey dragon. A khaki oval formed the background on battledress insignia: this was probably omitted on vehicles. **13** 4th Inf Div: dark grey grenade with red flames. **14** 5th Inf Div: light brown bison, yellow field. **15** 6th Inf Div: red/blue shield. **16** 7th Inf Div: red griffin, gold beak & claws. **Figs 17-20** described in text.

5   Regimental insignia

Not painted on vehicles, but see section 3 for regimental pennants.

6   Arm of service markings

Basically these followed the British system, but there were variations. In the interests of accuracy the entire arm of service flashes and unit serial numbers used by 1st Armoured Div in north-west Europe have been listed in **Table 16** rather than just refer the reader to the relevant British section.

7   Tactical markings

Tactical markings on AFV turrets followed the British system of a diamond for HQ, triangle for 1st Sqdn, square for 2nd, and circle for 3rd: numbers not letters were used for sqdns in Polish regts. In 1st Armoured Div all these signs were painted in white.

8   Call signs

As British system.

9   Vehicle names

AFVs of 1st Armoured Div rarely carried names: two rare examples are *Kitus II* (HQ Sqdn 2nd Armoured Regt), and *Hela* (CinC's tank, 1st Armoured Div). The AFVs of 2nd Armoured Div, on the other hand, had names more often than not, usually painted in white on the applique armour on the hull sides of Shermans. The following examples are all from Shermans of the div, and are either the names of girls, towns, battles, or famous Polish leaders: *Helunia, Bohun, Taza-Khurma, Tobruk, Quassasin, Hill-69, Rycerzi, Przeboj, Quizil-Ribat, Piedimonte, Bdynia.*

Plate XXI: Polish formation signs.

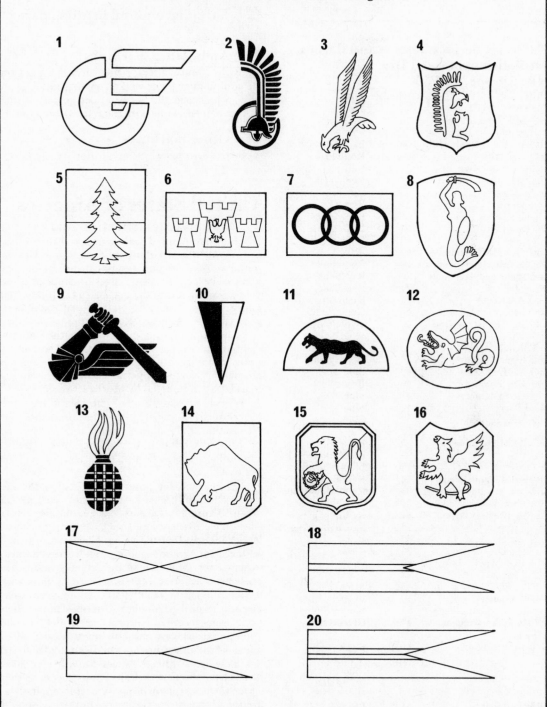

10   Vehicle serial numbers

As British systems.

Table 16: Serial numbers and flashes, 1st Polish Armoured Div, NW Europe, 1944-5.

Unit	Number	Flash
Div HQ	40	Black
HQ 10th Armoured Cav Bde	50	Red
HQ 3rd Rifles Bde	60	Light green
HQ Div Arty	40	Red/blue
1st Armoured Regt	51	Red
2nd Armoured Regt	52	Red
24th Lancers	53	Red
10th Drgns	54	Red
Highland Rifle Bn	61	Light green
8th Rifles Bn	62	Light green
9th Rifles Bn	63	Light green
1st Indep HMG Sqdn	64	Black
1st Motorised Arty Regt	74	Red/blue
2nd Motorised Arty Regt	76	Red/blue
1st A/T Regt	77	Red/blue
1st LAA Regt	73	Red/blue
10th Mounted Rifles	45	Green/blue
HQ Signals, 1st and 2nd Sqdns	40	White/blue
3rd Signals Sqdn	60	White/blue
10th Signals Sqdn	50	White/blue
HQ Div Engineers	40	Blue
10th Coy Engineers	46	Blue
11th Coy Engineers	41	Blue
Field Park	42	Blue
Div Bridging unit	52 Br	Blue
HQ REME (equivalent)	40	Blue/yellow/red
10th Coy	99	Blue/yellow/red
3rd Coy	100	Blue/yellow/red
HQ RASC (equivalent)	80	Red/light green
3rd Coy	83	Red/light green
10th Coy	81	Red/light green
Div Supply Coy	84	Red/light green
Inf Transport Coy	85	Red/light green
1st Field Hygiene Pl	89	Black
1st Field Dressing Sta	90	Black
10th Light Medical Coy	92	Black
11th Medical Coy	93	Black
1st Traffic Control Sqdn	43	Black
HQ Ordnance	40	Blue/red/blue
1st Field Ordnance Park	97	Blue/red/blue
1st Tank Replacement Sqdn	473	Green/blue
Replenishment unit	1102	Black with white bars across top and diagonally
Field Post unit	44	Black

11   Bridge classification numbers

As British systems.

12   Shipping and rail loading marks

As British systems.

13   Ambulance markings

As British ambulances. One variant occurs on the ambulance Jeeps of 2nd Armoured Div in Italy, which had the entire upper surface of the bonnet painted white with the red cross overall.

14   Other markings

As British systems where applicable.

United States of America

1   National identification marks

A white five-pointed star with a red disc at the centre and on a circular blue background was the national identification symbol in use before the USA entered the war, and it appeared on vehicles until *at least* the end of 1941. It does not appear to have been revised until new regulations were issued in August 1942:

'A white five-pointed star will be the national symbol of all motor vehicles assigned to tactical units. Administrative motor vehicles operating in an active theatre of operations will be similarly marked when directed by the theatre cmdrs.

'Whenever requirements for camouflage and concealment outweigh the requirements for recognition, the national symbol may be covered by lusterless olive-drab gasoline solvent paint, camouflage nets, oil and dirt, etc, or will be removed.'

Gasoline solvent paint was specified for the star itself, and official locations and sizes are set out in **Table 17**. Despite this regulation, white stars on circular coloured backgrounds continued to be used, and examples have been seen as late as the Sicily landing, July 1943. No concrete evidence on the colour of these backgrounds has yet been found, but it was either red or blue, with the latter as the most likely. These coloured backgrounds were particularly noticeable on US vehicles operating in North Africa in 1942-3.

New regulations issued in February 1945 made slight amendments to size and location, and now gave official details for those vehicles introduced since 1942. They also specified that white lusterless stencilling synthetic enamel be used, and that on vertical surfaces the star should appear with a single point uppermost, and on horizontal surfaces with a single point directed towards the rear of the vehicle.

No mention is made in the regulations of any other markings, but three types of white markings were commonly used in conjunction with the white star: **1.** A thick white band round the turrets of AFVs during 1942-3, appearing on AFVs in North Africa, the south-west Pacific, and units training in the UK and USA. **2.** A thick white circle round the star, broken at each of the star's points, appearing on vehicles throughout 1943-5 and in all theatres, though to a considerably less extent in the Pacific. **3.** A continuous thick white circle round the star, touching at each point, appearing as for 2.

In north-west Europe and Italy the last two versions were used almost entirely on horizontal surfaces as aerial recognition signs, though by no means all stars in such positions had the circles round them. In the Pacific theatre the US Marine Corps used only the official plain white star.

The national flag was also used on occasion as a national identification symbol, painted on the sides of softskins' bonnets and on the hull fronts and sides of tanks. It was widely used for the Operation Torch landings in North Africa, but occurs only on rare occasions thereafter: its use was apparently only ever official for Operation Torch. See also section 10 for the USA prefix to vehicle serial numbers.

Table 17: US Army national identification sizes and locations.

Vehicle	Location	Diameter in/cms
Motor cycles	Gas tank sides, rear and sides of sidecars	6/15.2
Cars	Centre of front bumper	4/10.1
	Rear side doors	20/50.6
	Rear	15/37.6
	Roof top (1945 regs)	36/90
Jeeps	Centre of front bumper	4/10.1
	Bonnet top	15/37.6
	Rear of sides	6/15.2
	Left of rear	12/30
Command cars	Centre of front bumper	4/10.1
	Bonnet top and rear of sides	15/37.6
	Centre of rear	10/25.3
Weapons Carriers	Centre of front bumper	
	½-ton	4/10.1
	¾-ton	6/15.2
	Bonnet top ½-ton	20/50.6
	¾- and ½-ton in 1945 regs	25/62.5
1½-ton cargo Trucks	Rear of sides ½-ton, Centre of sides ¾-ton, centre of rear on both	10/25.3
	Centre of front bumper	6/15.2
	Bonnet top { open cab	20/50.6
	{ closed cab	25/62.5
	Cab doors	25/62.5
	Cab sides, open cab	15/37.6
	Cab roof, closed cab only	36/90
	Centre of tailboard	10/25.3
	Left rear mudguard	16/34.1
2½-ton cargo trucks	Centre of front bumper	6/15.2
	Bonnet top on open cab, cab roof on closed cab	32/80.3
	Cab doors	25/62.5
	Cab sides on open cab	15/37.6
	Centre of tailboard	10/25.3
	Left rear mudguard	16/34.1
4-ton cargo trucks	Centre of front bumper	6/15.2
	Bonnet top and cab doors	25/62.5
	Cab roof	32/80.3
	Centre of tailboard	10/25.3
	Left rear mudguard	15/37.6
Scout cars and ½-tracks	Centre of radiator and sides	20/50.6
	Bonnet top	36/90
	Centre of rear	15/37.6
Light tanks	Turret sides and top	20/50.6
	Centre of hull rear	10/25.3
	Hull sides (1945 regs)	16/34.1
Medium tanks	Turret sides, rear and top	20/50.6
	Top of engine decks (M3)	36/90
Added by 1945 regulations:		
M8 armoured cars	Turret sides, hull sides aft, hull rear and front	16/34.1
	Top of engine decks	36/90
Priest SP gun	Fighting compartment sides	20/50.6
	Glacis	25/62.5
	Left and right rear	16/34.1 or 20/50.6
Grants	Turret top	20/50.6
	Centre of hull front	25/62.5
	Centre of hull rear	16/34.1
	Top of engine decks	36/90
Shermans	Turret top	20/50.6
	Glacis	25/62.5
	Top of engine decks	60/152
Tank destroyers	Glacis	36/90
	Hull sides and rear	20/50.6
	Top of engine decks	45/113

2 Aerial recognition symbols

A five-pointed white star on horizontal surfaces as described in full in section 1.

3 Rank, signal and other flags

Vehicles used by general officers officially carried a metal plate 6 in (15.2 cm) high by 9 in (22.8 cm) long on the front right wing or bumper and left rear bumper. The plate was removed or covered when the general officer was not in the vehicle. The plate was painted red and bore white five-pointed stars: one for Brigadier General, two for Major General, three for Lieutenant General, four for General (or Commandant USMC), and five for General of the Army. In practise cloth flags were sometimes used on the front of vehicles in place of the plates, flown from short rods at the front right wing. The flags appear most often on cars: plates were always used on AFVs.

4 Formation signs

Formation signs were painted on vehicles as a means of unit identification in World War 1, between the wars, and right up until the USA entered World War 2. They were replaced by unit codes in 1942. Numerous examples of formation signs on vehicles of all types occur until the end of 1941, but thereafter their use was normally limited to staff cars and Jeeps of Army, Corps and Div cmdrs. In these cases the signs normally—and officially—appeared on metal plates 6 in high (15.2 cm) by 9 in (22.8 cm) wide, positioned at front right and left rear on the vehicles. They were used together with the unit codes, not in place of them.

Because formation signs were not used on combat vehicles, and because the signs of higher formations have been illustrated elsewhere many times, for space reasons the Army, Corps and Div formation signs have not been included amongst the illustrations in this book. Readers are referred to E.E. Kerrigan's excellent book, *American Badges and Insignia*.

5 Regimental insignia

The use of distinctive insignia (or regimental 'crests') had been widespread pre-war, and their use remained common during 1940-1. They still appeared quite frequently on vehicles during 1942 and even 1943, but from the beginning of 1944 their usage declined sharply. However, their appearance on vehicles during 1944-5 was still common enough to warrant coverage here, particularly on the vehicles of arty and cav units and independent coys and bns, even though the signs rarely appeared on AFVs. This 'unofficial' insignia usually appeared on vehicle sides, and was normally in colour, though one isolated example of a simplified regt insignia, presumably being used as a tactical marking, has been seen stencilled in white on the front bumpers of softskins of that regt: see the accompanying

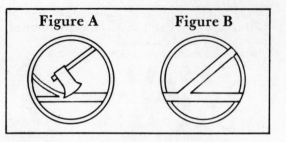

figure, a) regt distinctive insignia, 84th Inf, red field, white axe and timber; b) simplified version painted on vehicles in north-west Europe, 1944-5. Examples of regt distinctives are illustrated in **Plates XXII-XXIV**.

Plate XXII (opposite): USA formation signs; 12th Armored Div.

September 15 1942-December 17 1945. All signs have yellow shading in the folds of the scrolls. **1** 23rd Tank Bn: red fleur de lis and heart, edged gold and with gold sprays below. **2** 43rd Tank Bn: gold and red flames and 'antlers'. **3** 714th Tank Bn: yellow shield, red spear tip. **4** 17th Armored Inf Bn: medium blue shield, lettering and scroll edging, pale blue device at top left. **5** 56th Armored Inf Bn: medium blue device at top left, lettering and scroll edging. **6** 66th Armored Inf Bn: medium blue device and scroll edging. **7** 493rd Armored FA Bn: red shield, lettering and scroll edging, gold devices. **8** 494th Armored FA Bn: yellow shield, weapon heads and six-pointed star, red 'flaming' chevron, weapon shafts and scroll edging. **9** 495th Armored FA Bn: red shield, lettering and scroll edging, yellow horse. **10** 92nd Cav Recce Sqdn: red tongue, lettering and scroll edging. **11** 119th Armored Engineer Bn: red lettering and scroll edging, and sinister side of shield. **12** 134th Armored Ordnance Bn: red shield, lettering and scroll edging, yellow cog with green centre and white bend.

Plate XXIII (page 59): USA formation signs.

1 152nd Armored Signal Coy: red hand and scroll. **2** 82nd Armored Medic Bn: reddish-brown shield, lettering and scroll edging. **3** 649th Engineer Topographic Bn: red shield and lettering. **4** 5th Medic Bn: upper half of shield red, yellow stars and scroll. **5** 248th Signals Bn: dark blue shield edged yellow. **6** 11th Ordnance Coy: red flame, yellow numeral and scroll. **7** 760th Transportation Bn: red shield, headline and beam in yellow. **8** 511th Engineer Separate Bn: red star and lower half of shield. **9** 321st Cav

Plate XXII: USA formation signs; 12th Armored Div.

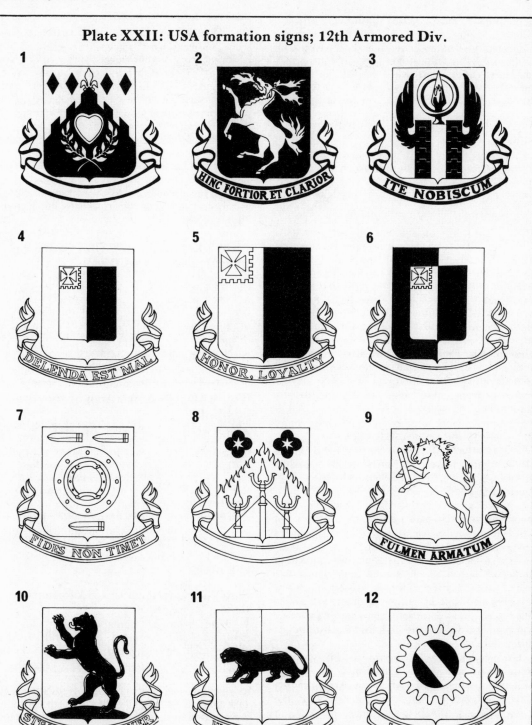

1

2 HINC FORTIOR ET CLARIOR

3 ITE NOBISCUM

4 DELENDA EST MAL

5 HONOR, LOYALTY

6

7 FIDES NON TIMET

8

9 FULMEN ARMATUM

10 STEALTH AND POWER

11 WORK AND FIGHT

12 I MAKE SURE

Regt: brown bear, green garland with red ribbon, gold scroll. **10** 30th Engineer Topographic Bn: red shield and lettering. **11** 156th FA Bn: blue over red shield, gold emblems, canton and shield edging, in canton red cross and blue saltire. **12** 308th QM Bn: buff shield, dark blue emblem, canton and lettering.

Plate XXIV (page 61): USA formation signs.

1 25th Armored Inf Bn: blue shield and lettering, gold scroll and shield edging, green palm tree, yellow trunk. **2** 36th Armored Inf Bn: green emblem edged gold, blue/gold wreath below. **3** 41st Armored Inf Bn: blue shield, two gold circles, in canton green six-bastioned fort. **4** 54th Armored Inf Bn: blue shield, edged and with bend in gold, green ladder, ragged brown tree stump. **5** 370th Armored Inf Bn: blue shield and lettering. **6** 373rd Armored Inf Bn: blue shield, orange fess edged gold. **7** 701st Armored Inf Bn: blue lion and lettering, gold fleur de lis. **8** 702nd Armored Inf Bn: yellow shield and lettering, red dinosaur and scroll. **9** 389th Tank Bn: gold shield and scroll, jayhawk in proper colours of blue/white/brown. **10** 601st Tank Destroyer Bn: gold field and stars. **11** 462nd Armored Car Sqdn: gold shield, grey bend flanked each side by two dark-blue stripes. **12** 761st Tank Bn: red mouth to panther.

6 Arm of service markings

All Army vehicles carried the term US ARMY or USA, applied in conjunction with the vehicle's serial number, and all US Marine Corps vehicles the term USMC or US MARINE CORPS on buses, ambulances and the like, which were not frontline vehicles and had large surfaces on which to display such markings. These markings are described in full in section 10.

Arm of service within the Army was indicated by a code letter, which formed part of the unit code system: in order not to confuse the reader, the entire unit code system is described under this heading instead of splitting it into its various components, which would fall under a number of different headings.

Unit codes were made up as follows: the number of the Army concerned in Arabic numerals, succeeded by an A for Army; or the Corps number in Roman numerals with the suffix AB if an Airborne Corps, or Δ if an armoured corps; or the Div number in Arabic numerals, also followed by AB if airborne or Δ if armoured. When applicable a Bde number was

used, in Arabic numerals, with the appendage BG. The same applied to Group numbers, which were followed by the letters GP. Some other codes at this higher level were: AGF Army Ground Forces, SOS Services of Supply, (not in 1945 regs), GHQ General Headquarters, RTC Replacement Training Centre preceded by arm of service symbol, and (in the 1945 regs) ASF Army Service Forces. Appropriate and non-conflicting letters were assigned to identify other formations as necessary, for example, TC Transport Corps, and AADC Army Air Defence Command.

Regt or bn codes followed the same pattern; a number for the regt, bn or detached coy; but in addition each unit number was followed by a branch of service symbol, see **Table 18**.

Battle Groups, recce sqdns, tank bns and FA bns operating under the regt system were identified by B, R and Δ respectively, preceded by their number in the usual manner and followed by the basic identification of the unit concerned. Where a unit had no intermediate organisation, or no special detached activity, and this most often applied at HQ level, then the letter X was used, for example: 1-X-HQ-10, 1st Inf Div, HQ Coy, 10th vehicle.

Table 18: US Army arm of service symbols.

Arm of service	Symbol	Remarks
Airborne	AB	
Army Air Force units	Star 3 in high	Changed to wings and propeller in 3 in diameter circle in 1945 regs.
Anti-aircraft	AA	
Amphibious	AM	Changed to APH in 1945 regs
Armoured units	Triangle 3 in high	Width of strokes ¼ in
Cavalry	C	
Chemical warfare	G	
Coast Arty Corps	CA	
Corps of Engineers	E	
Field Arty	F	
Inf	I	Preceded by ½ in dash
Medical Dept	M	
Military Police	P	
Mountain	—	MN added in 1945 regs
Ordnance Dept	O	Preceded by ½ in dash
QM Corps	Q	
Signal Corps	S	
Tank destroyer units	TD	
Tank Grp	TG	Not listed in 1945 regs

Plate XXIII: USA formation signs.

1

RESOLUTE TO ACHIEVE

2

CELERE AD CONSERVATIONEM

3

PATHFINDERS

4

IN BELLO MISERICORDIA

5

ALWAYS TALKING

6

11

PERAGIMUS OMNI

7

RECTE FERIO

8

9

TIENS TA FOI

10

IMPRIMIS

11

12

PRIDE IN PERFORMANCE

At the lowest level the codes operated as before, using coy or btty letters, with HQ for Headquarters and Headquarters units, and SV for service units. Coys operating independently also carried a code to identify their role, see **Table 19**. Units with roles not covered by these codes could invent appropriate ones, provided they did not exceed three letters, for example, TMP, Transportation Motor Pool. Each vehicle within a unit was assigned a number in the sequence in which that vehicle would normally appear in the order of march. Towed trailers were counted as separate vehicles and allocated a number directly following that of the towing vehicle. Thus 1-10 were normally allocated to the HQ unit of a coy, 11-20 to vehicles of the 1st Platoon, 21-30 to vehicles of 2nd Platoon, and so on. B-11 would therefore be the first vehicle of the 1st Platoon of Coy B.

The following examples of unit codes used during World War 2 should help to clarify the system in the reader's mind: 1-X-1S-10: 10th vehicle, 1st Signal Coy, 1st Inf Div. 1-33F-D-8: 8th vehicle, Btty D, 33rd FA Bn, 1st Inf Div. 1-1E-A-4: 4th vehicle, Coy A, 1st Engineer Bn, 1st Inf Div. 1Δ-1Q-A-8: 8th vehicle, Coy A, Supply Bn, 1st Armoured Div. 1Δ-6-I-A-2: 2nd vehicle, Coy A, 6th Inf Bn, 1st Armoured Div. 1C-12C-HQ-7: 7th vehicle, HQ Troop, 12th Cav, 1st Cav Div. 1C-1M-A-10: 10th vehicle, Troop A, 1st Medic Sqdn, 1st Cav Div. 2A-21Q-A-3: 3rd vehicle, Coy A, 21st QM Regt, 2nd Army. ☆-1Q-SVAV-8: 8th vehicle, 1st QM Coy, Service Group (AVn) Army Air Forces. II-3M-EV-5: 5th vehicle, 3rd Evacuation Hospital, II Corps. 3A-X-60-0-10: 10th vehicle, 60th Ordnance Coy, 3rd Army. I-1FOB-A-4: 4th vehicle, Btty A, 1st FA Observation Bn, I Corps.

The codes were painted in white directly on to the olive-drab of the vehicles, in the largest size possible (up to 4 in (10.2 cm) high maximum,

but governed by the surface area available) and appeared on front and rear (rear only of trailers). Stencils were used whenever possible, but the codes could be hand-painted at the discretion of the unit cmdr.

Officially the first two groups of code symbols were to be removed when leaving for theatres of operations or ports of embarkation: the 1945 regulations stipulate that merely painting over the codes was not acceptable. *All* codes had to be removed or obliterated when, 'requirements for camouflage and concealment outweigh the requirements for recognition' using the methods listed for national identification marks in section 1. Despite this, *full* unit codes continued to appear on all types of vehicles, including some AFVs in the front line, until the end of the war, although they are frequently obliterated by the censor in war-time photographs.

7 Tactical markings

The August 1942 regulations set out the system of tactical markings precisely, and it is worth quoting them in full here:

'Tactical Markings: a) Divs, separate bdes, combat commands, combat teams, similar separate unit cmdrs, and higher unit cmdrs may prescribe a system of tactical markings for units of their commands. This may include the naming of individual vehicles. b) Tactical markings will be painted on vehicles using gasoline solvent paint or paints approved by the War Dept. Colours may be used. The HQs directing use of tactical marking will specify the location of tactical marking. c) Tactical markings may consist of stripes, geometrical figures, combinations of geometrical figures, or combinations of geometrical figures and shapes. d) Tactical markings will be of such a size as to make ground to ground identification of vehicles possible. e) Tactical markings will be removed when camouflage or concealment outweighs the requirements for recognition. f) (1) The system of tactical markings prescribed will in no way represent the numerical designation or the distinctive insignia of any unit. (2) In a combat zone, the system of tactical markings will be changed whenever conditions require. (3) In a theatre of operations, no written record will be made or published of the system of tactical markings.'

Of course, the last proviso effectively rules out any chance of definitely locating most of the various tactical markings used during the war, or identifying the units employing them. However, much can be deduced from photographs, and I have been fortunate in receiving information

---

Table 19: US Army coy codes

Role	Symbol	Remarks
Ammunition	—	AM added in 1945 regs
Anti-tank	AT	
Cannon	CN	
Depot	—	DP added in 1945 regs
Heavy Weapons	HW	
Maintenance	MT	
Mortar	—	MR added in 1945 regs
Recce	R	
Rocket	—	RT added in 1945 regs
Train	TN	
Weapons	W	

Plate XXIV: USA formation signs.

1. ONWARD

2.

3. STRAIGHT AND STALWART

4.

5. POWER TO STRIKE

6. PERFORM THE TASK

7. GALLANTLY FORWARD

8. MEMOR ESTO

9. FIGHTING HAWK

10.

11.

12. COME OUT FIGHTING

from a number of men who served in World War 2. Detailed and accurate information is limited, and that which has been discovered to date deals only with geometrical shapes. It is listed in **Plate XXV.**

These geometric signs were usually painted on turret or hull sides on AFVs, and on the front bumper of half-tracks and softskins. Single digit numbers were used in 1st Armoured Div in Tunisia to distinguish platoons within a coy, and were painted in black on or alongside the tactical sign.

Other systems of markings included a single or double letter, two- or on rare occasions three-digit numbers, and combinations of letters and numbers, such as A-33 (Sherman), D-3 (M-8 armoured car), DT-7 (Sherman bulldozer), G-34 (Sherman) and so on. These were all in white on the turret or hull sides, and as large as the surface allowed. In the Pacific theatre more complex combinations sometimes appeared, such as 1-C-8, 5-C-4, seen on Amtracs at Emirau in March 1944.

Abbreviated titles were also used by some motor transport units, despite the official regulations. They were normally painted in white on cab doors, and were totally unnecessary, as the unit codes revealed the identity of any vehicle. An example is 13th QM B Co B (13th QM Bn, Coy B). Other examples may be seen in Vanderveen's *The Observer's Fighting Vehicles Directory.*

A unique system of tactical markings was employed in the Pacific theatre by the US Marine Corps. A basic symbol was assigned to each div: it is believed these were not changed during the war, but they were assigned to different divs when used again in the Korean War, and were changed for each year's manoeuvres thereafter. The signs were: 1st Marine Div, a triangle; 2nd, not known but probably a square; 3rd, a diamond; 4th, a half circle; 5th, a rectangle; 6th, a circle. Inside the symbol were placed three numbers: 1st, a number assigned to each regt and the divisional troops within a div; 2nd, the bn's own number; 3rd, a number for the coy, starting with HQ as 1, and the coys following in numerical order so Coy A was always 2, Coy B 3, etc. Therefore, it is necessary to know the numbers assigned to each regt and to div troops to identify vehicles, but unfortunately this part of my information is incomplete. Known numbers are listed below:

1st Marine Div: 6 = 11th Marine Regt (Arty). *3rd Marine Div:* 1 = Div HQ Bn; 2 = unknown; 3 = 3rd Marine Regt; 4 = 9th Marine Regt; 5

= 21st Marine Regt; 6 = 12th Marine Regt (Arty). *4th Marine Div:* 1 = Div HQ Bn; 2 = 23rd Marine Regt; 3 = 24th Marine Regt; 4 = 25th Marine Regt; 5 = 20th Marine Regt (Engineers), 1943-early 1944 only; 6 = 14th Marine Regt (Arty); *5th Marine Div:* 1 = Div HQ Bn; 2 = unknown; 3 = 26th Marine Regt; 4 = 27th Marine Regt; 5 = 28th Marine Regt; 6 = 13th Marine Regt (Arty).

It is possible, but not known for sure, that the blank numbers (2 in 3rd and 5th Divs) were allocated to the divisional troops. Therefore, the Engineers, Service, Motor Transport, Medical, Amphibious tractor, Tank and Pioneer Bns would all have used 2 as their first number, followed by their own bn and coy numbers as usual.

An example of the Marine code system is 641 within a diamond = 1st Marine Div (diamond), 11th Marine Regt (6), 4th Bn (4), HQ Coy (1).

The markings were usually about 6 by 3 in (15.2 by 7.6 cm) in size and were stencilled on the left or right side of front and rear bumpers of vehicles. It is believed that the system did not come into use until 1943, and that it was supposed to be applied to all vehicles. However, the Marines were more security conscious than the Army, and few vehicles in the front line bore any markings at all. Marine AFVs normally carried a two figure number, or single figure number within a geometrical shape, painted in white on the sides and rear of turrets, and often repeated on the hull rear.

The Army regulations issued in February 1945 laid down one further restriction on tactical markings, namely:

'The decoration of organisational equipment (including motor vehicles) with individual characteristic designs such as caricatures, cartoons, coats of arms, and symbolic figures is not authorised.' This was no doubt provoked by the popularity with vehicle crews of pin-ups, Disney characters and the like, and the occasional continued use of regimental crests. Such designs appear on all manner of vehicles, usually on hull sides or cab doors, and were sometimes in colour. Although not strictly speaking tactical markings, they did serve to identify individual vehicles within a sub-unit.

Plate XXV (opposite): USA tactical markings.

Figs 1-4, 1st Armored Regt, 1st Armored Div, Tunisian campaign. **1** Combat Command A HQ. **2** 1st Bn: HQ Coy, A, B and C Coys. **3** 2nd Bn: HQ Coy, A, B and C Coys. **4** 3rd Bn: HQ

Plate XXV: USA tactical markings.

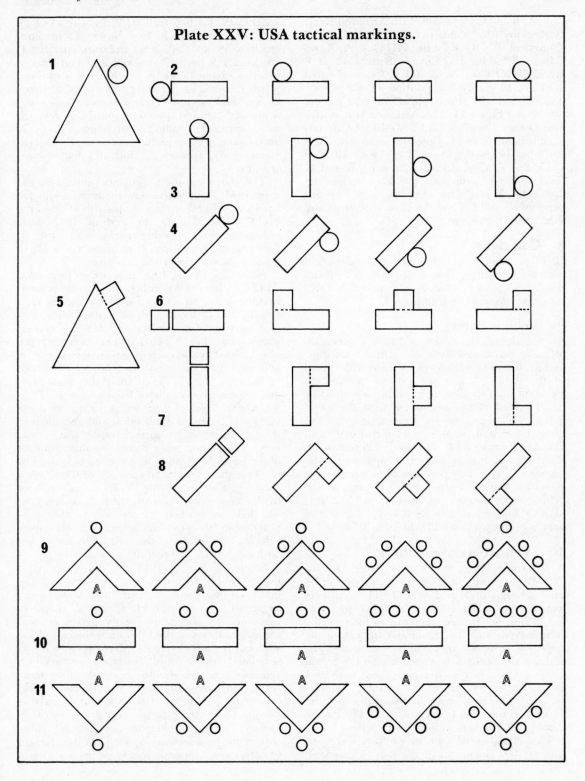

Coy, A, B and C Coys. **5-8**, 13th Armored Regt, 1st Armored Div, Tunisian campaign. **5** Combat Command 'B' HQ. **6** 1st Bn: HQ Coy, A, B and C Coys. **7** 2nd Bn: HQ Coy, A, B and C Coys. **8** 3rd Bn: HQ Coy, A, B and C Coys. (Dotted lines are to clarify the position of the square symbol and did not appear on the actual markings.) **Figs 9-11**, 12th Armored Div, north-west Europe 1944-5. **9** 23rd Tank Bn: A Coy 1st-5th Platoons; B and C Coys the same with their coy letter below the inverted chevron. **10** 43rd Tank Bn: A Coy, 1st-5th Platoons; B and C Coys the same with their coy letter below the dash. **11** 714th Tank Bn: A Coy, 1st-5th Platoons; B and C Coys the same with their coy letter above the chevron.

8   Call signs

Call signs as such are not amongst the numerical tactical markings described in the official regulations, and it is therefore assumed that this type of marking was not employed.

9   Vehicle names

As mentioned in section 7, names were an officially recognised form of tactical markings, and the use of names on vehicles was widespread in the Army. It has not proved possible to ascertain whether all vehicles within a platoon or coy received names beginning with the same letter on all occasions, but they appear to have done so on some occasions, ie, Fire Buggy and Flaming Fanny, Betty Sue and Baton Rouge. Place names, battles, famous people and girls' names were especially popular. Most names were stencilled, and were frequently as large as the vehicle serial number, ie, up to 4 in (10.2 cm) high. White paint was used, and the names normally appeared on hull sides or cab doors.

10   Vehicle serial numbers

A serial numbering system was introduced for War Dept vehicles in 1929 and continued to be used throughout World War 2. The numbers were formed from 1st, the letter W for War Dept; 2nd, one or two numerals to indicate the vehicle type; and 3rd, a number indicating the sequence in which the vehicle was issued. In addition the prefix K was used by the US Signal Corps for special vehicle types. From mid-1944 on the prefix W was often omitted. Vehicles supplied to US Forces in Australia by the Australian motor industry for use in the Pacific theatre had numbers with the prefix letter U.

The official serial number prefixes were:- 0, trailers; 00, maintenance trucks; 1, cars and sedans; 10, kitchen trailers; 2, light trucks to 1 ton; 20, recce trucks and buses; 3, medium trucks to 1½ ton; 30, tanks and some specials; 4, trucks 2½-5 ton; 40, tracked and half-tracked vehicles except tanks; 5, trucks over 5 ton and prime movers; 50, fire and crash trucks; 6, motor cycles and motor cycle combinations; 60, armoured cars and special technical vehicles such as command, radio, searchlight, etc; 7, ambulances; 70, amphibious vehicles; 8, wheeled tractors; 80, tankers; 9, full and half-tracked tractors.

The above numbers were the prefixes in use from 1943. Prior to this date the terminology for trucks was slightly different, and this affected the prefix codes. Up to the end of 1942 these variations were: 2, utility trucks ¾ to 1 ton; 3, light trucks 1¼ to 2 ton; 4, medium trucks 2½ to 4 ton; 5, heavy trucks 5 ton and over.

According to the 1942 regulations (amended April 22) the serial numbers were to be painted in blue-drab lusterless enamel by means of a stencil, 1 in (2.5 cm) high on motor cycles, 2 in (5.1 cm) high on trailers and US registration plates, and 4 in (10.2 cm) high on all other types of vehicles. Location was to be:- on passenger cars and metropolitan ambulances: under the hood, on the right side, in the centre of the upper part, and on registration plates front and rear. Field ambulances, panel and sedan vans: on outer surface of the hood, both sides, and also the rear doors. Motor cycles: on registration plates, rear only. Trucks and recce trucks: on outer surface of the hood, both sides, and also on tailgate. For trucks without hoods, on each end of the driver's seat, and also on tailgate. Trailers: in centre of the back. Combat vehicles, tracked, wheeled, or wheeled and tracked: to conform as closely as practicable to marking prescribed for other vehicles. (In practice this normally meant on both sides, front and rear of the vehicle.)

Sometime during 1943 the blue-drab paint began to be phased out as it rendered the markings too inconspicuous, and white paint began to be used instead. Blue-drab numbers continued to appear on many prototype and training vehicles in the USA until the end of the war, but in the February 1945 regulations it was stipulated that white lusterless, stencilling, synthetic enamel should be used. The same regulations now stated the numbers should appear on both sides of the hood, 'as nearly as possible on a vertical panel but near the top of the hood so as to be visible from the side, and on the rear of the vehicle when space permits.' Height of letters and numerals was to be from 1 to 4 in

(2.5 to 10.2 cm), the largest size practicable being used.

On Army vehicles the serial number was preceded by the legend USA or US ARMY. Normally this appeared in a separate line above the registration number, but legend and number could be painted in a single line if there was room. The prefix followed the same size and paint colour specifications as for serial numbers.

In the USMC all vehicles carried the legend USMC in the same size, paint colour and locations as for the Army. The Marine Corps used an entirely different serial number system, without the prefix codes, but I have been unable to identify any regularity in the numbering: it would seem the numbers represent only the sequence in which the vehicles were issued for service with the Corps, the sequence being commenced separately for different classes of vehicles.

11 Bridge classification numbers

No system is mentioned in the 1942 regulations but sometime during 1943 the Army adopted the British system of bridge classification numbers. However, the February 1945 regulations enumerate an individual US system, with the weight class painted in black on an 8 in (20.3 cm) square or 8 by 6 in (20.3 by 15.2 cm) rectangular metal plate. Vehicles with bumpers carried this plate on the front bumper, right of centre; AFVs on the front of the hull level with the top of the tracks or wheels; trailers on the right side near the front; towed guns on the trail; half-tracks and scout cars on the forward edge of the right fender; and amphibious trucks on the front right. No class numbers are listed, but weight class numbers were to show the gross loaded weight of a tractor or prime-mover *and* its tow. Thus a towing vehicle carried the gross weight of tow and towing vehicle over or preceding the gross weight of towing vehicle alone: $\frac{7}{5}$ or 7/5 (1½-ton truck with trailer). Known bridge class numbers are: 2, Jeep or trailer; 4, ¾-ton ambulance; 5, 1½-ton truck; 7, M8 armoured car; 10, 2½-ton truck; 15, Stuart tank; 16, M18 tank destroyer; 30, Sherman; and 34, Pershing tank.

However, I have not seen any examples of these square or rectangular plates in war-time photographs, and it would appear the British system was followed until the end of the war, at least in the European theatre. Further information on the system may therefore be found in the British section 11.

12 Shipping and rail loading marks

All vehicles shipped overseas had a data panel giving in abbreviated form the external dimension of the vehicle in inches, and its shipping and combat weight in pounds, plus other details relevant to the particular vehicle. The panel, consisting of up to five lines, was painted as a block, ie, each line below the preceding one, on each side of the vehicle and in a convenient position. Usually the lettering was painted in 1 or 2 in (2.5 or 5.1 cm) high white lettering straight on to the olive-drab finish, but occasionally the area was over-painted as a matt black panel before the lettering was applied.

13 Ambulance markings

The instructions given in the 1942 regulations are quoted in full here, as they give the precise information required: there were no changes in the 1945 regulations.

'Both sides of the body of an ambulance will be marked with a Geneva cross, bright red, on a snowy-white field, the cross to be 18 in (45 cm) in the horizontal and vertical dimensions and each limb to represent a 6 in (15.2 cm) square. It will be located in the centre of the middle or advertising panel of the body. A Geneva cross on a snow-white field will be placed in the centre of the top and on the outside. This cross will be of such size that the transverse arm will reach entirely across the top. On the visor, or directly above the windshield, will be marked in suitable size white letters, block style, the word AMBULANCE. On each side of the word AMBULANCE will be placed a small bright-red Geneva cross on a white field, or two small red Geneva crosses may be placed on either side of the windshield in a location that will not interfere with the operator's vision. On the perpendicular centre line of each of the rear doors, below the windows, will be placed a 6 in (15.2 cm) bright-red Geneva cross on an 8 in (20.3 cm) white field. All lettering executed in white will be properly shaded to give depth.

'A caduceus, the insignia of the Medical Department, in maroon, will be painted on both sides of the body of an ambulance below the lower moulding and 7 in (17.7 cm) to the rear of the front body as follows: a caduceus 6 in (15.2 cm) in height outlined with a narrow white stripe will be painted with its anterior edge 7 in (17.7 cm) from the rear edge of the side door. Two in (5.1 cm) below this caduceus in 1 in (2.5 cm) white letters, block style, in two lines, will be painted the words UNITED STATES/ARMY. All paints to be lusterless synthetic enamel.'

14 Other markings

Convoy markings: A visibility patch of three vertical white stripes and four alternate black ones, forming a rectangle, was frequently painted on the rear fender or similar low position at the rear of vehicles to act as a station-keeping aid to drivers in the column of march or in convoys.

Explosives: Vehicles carrying explosives exhibited the word EXPLOSIVES in white letters not less than 3 in (7.6 cm) high on a red placard at the front, rear and both sides. In addition all bumpers were painted red.

Fuel tankers: The 1945 regulations stipulated that, 'Fuel serving trucks and trailers assigned to or operated by the Army Air Forces for the purpose of refuelling aircraft will bear special markings using black letters and numerals on vehicles painted chrome yellow, and white letters and numerals on vehicles painted olive-drab. The special markings will consist of the following: 1) (Grade or type) OCTANE GASOLINE, 2) NO SMOKING WITHIN 50 FEET'

Left-hand drive: All Army vehicles sent to the UK had painted in a prominent position on the rear CAUTION/LEFT HAND/DRIVE, or LEFT HAND/DRIVE/NO SIGNALS in letters 2 or 3 in (5.1 or 7.5 cm) high. This marking was usually retained during any subsequent shipping of the vehicle to Europe.

Maximum speed: A maximum speed sign often appeared on the front of vehicles, just below the windscreen. It consisted of the maximum specified speed preceded by MAX SPEED, all in 1 in (2.5 cm) high letters and numerals, in the same colour paint as was used for the vehicle's serial number.

Military police: All Jeeps used by the MPs carried the title MILITARY POLICE in 3 in (7.5 cm) high black letters round the circumference of a 16 in (40.2 cm) white disc which fitted into the centre of the spare wheel on the rear of the vehicle. The same title, and of the same size, was painted just below the vehicle's windscreen, and also across the canvas part of motorcycle windscreens, either in white or in black on a white band.

Radio interference suppression: The letter S was stencilled on both left and right sides of the hood, near the windscreen, of all vehicles fitted with radio interference suppression. The S normally appeared at the end of the serial number, frequently separated from it by a dash to avoid confusion, and was in the same colour and of the same height as the serial number.

Union of Soviet Socialist Republics

The Soviets are notoriously tight-lipped when it comes to revealing any details of their military forces—no matter how obsolete that information may now be—and the official markings carried on their vehicles during the Great Patriotic War are apparently still rated as restricted information: of the numerous letters sent by myself over the past decade to the Central Museum of the Armed Forces of the USSR in Moscow, not one has received a reply. Consequently *all* the information on Soviet markings listed below has been drawn entirely from photographic evidence.

As almost all Soviet vehicle markings were of a tactical nature, allocated by local cmdrs at a low level of command, it is doubtful if any precise system or systems were ever followed throughout the USSR's massive armies. Therefore, what follows is also largely a matter of opinion, and even the individual markings quoted as examples may be misinterpretations due to the poor quality of some of the photographs studied and my own lack of knowledge of the Russian language.

1 National identification marks

The five-pointed red star of the USSR was used as a national identification mark on vehicles throughout the war, either on the turret or hull sides of AFVs or, less often, on the glacis plate or even front wing. Lorries also carried the star on cab doors from at least mid-1944. Examples of the star in use at the front are rare in the early campaigns, but do occur quite frequently during the 1944-5 period. However, its use on front line vehicles was never widespread, and it was always more prolific on parade vehicles. The star sometimes had a narrow white edging, and in the last year of the war was on occasion painted all in white or with a thick white outline.

2 Aerial recognition symbols

A number of different types of aerial recognition symbols were used during the war, apparently laid down at a local level and used for only a limited length of time. Before the war cyrillic letters in white had been used on AFV turret tops, or thick white bands which encircled the top edges of the turret sides and lapped over on to the turret top to encircle the edges of that also. Some examples of these symbols occur in the early campaigns, but they are not seen during 1942. A large white cross was also used on the turret tops of some BT-7s and BA-10s at the beginning of the war.

Both the white crosses and white bands reappeared on AFV turret roofs and sides in 1943, but some of the white turret bands were now broken, being perhaps 3 in (7.5 cm) deep by 5 in (12.7 cm) long, and separated by gaps also 5 in long. These dotted bands occur on T-26s, T-38 amphibious tanks, BT-5(V) cmdrs' tanks, and on all three turrets of T-35s. On some BT-5s and T-35s there is a second, continuous white band above the broken one.

The broad white cross on turret roofs and thick white band, now round the *middle* of turret sides, were made official in April 1945 for all AFVs in the Berlin theatre, where co-operation with the Allied air forces made a standard system

essential. However, even at this late date, not *all* AFVs carried aerial recognition symbols, and their use seems to have been erratic throughout the war.

3 Rank, signal and other flags
No information, except small hand flags were used for communication purposes between tanks in the early years of the war (up to and including part of 1943) when few AFVs had radios.

4 Formation signs
A limited number of signs have been identified as peculiar to specific units and may be likened to the UK and USA formation signs. All the known examples are listed in **Plate XXVI**: they were all painted on turret sides in solid white. Such markings first appeared in 1942, but they were

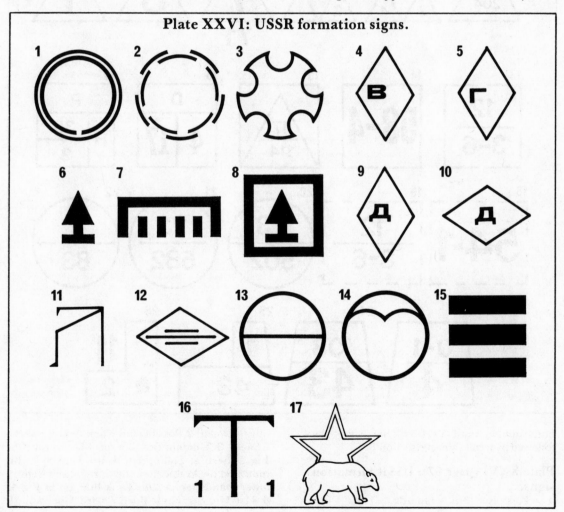

Plate XXVI: USSR formation signs.

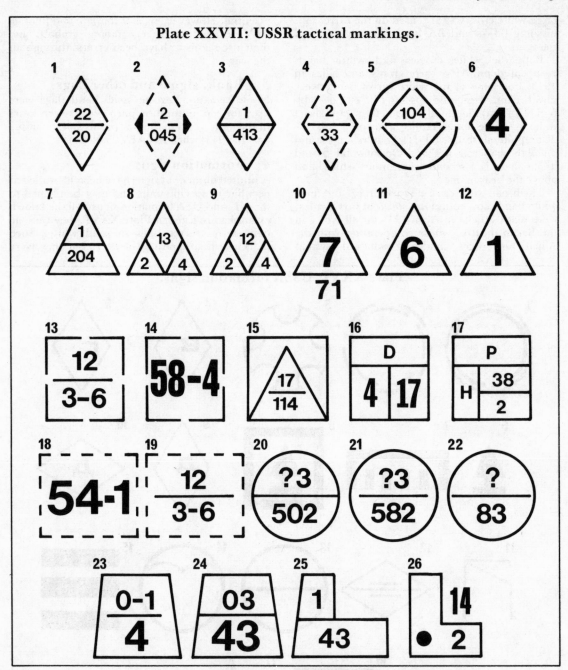

Plate XXVII: USSR tactical markings.

not common until 1944-5. They were always followed by a call sign; see section 8.

Plate XXVI (page 67): USSR formation signs.

1 Possibly 3rd Guards Tank Army: unconfirmed. **2** Possibly 5th Tank Army; unconfirmed. **3** Unidentified but possibly variant of **Fig 2**. Seen at Stalingrad. **4** 3rd Tank Bde, bn indicated by Arabic numeral to right and slightly lower than letter. **5** 39th Tank Bde, bn as **Fig 4**. **6** 41st Guards Tank Bde. **7** 63rd Chelyabinsk

Tank Bde. **8** 64th Guards Tank Bde. **9** 135th Tank Bde, bn as **Figs 4** and **5**. **10** 78th Guards Heavy Tank Regt. **11** 366th Guards Heavy SP Arty Regt. **12** 1443rd SP Arty Regt. **13-16** Unidentified units. **17** Unidentified unit within 4th Guards Tank Army, Berlin, 1945.

5   Regimental insignia
No information, except as illustrated in **Plate XXVI**.

6   Arm of service markings
Not used.

7   Tactical markings
The majority of AFVs carried some form of tactical marking throughout the war, almost always painted in white on the turret sides. Black was used on rare occasions, usually when a vehicle had been over-painted white for winter camouflage, but more often than not the white tactical markings were simply obliterated until the lime wash was removed with the thaw.

So far as can be interpreted from photographic evidence, there was a general system of tactical markings based on geometrical shapes and numbers. It would appear this system was administered at a local level. Examples are given in **Plate XXVII** and from these it can be seen that most numbers could be interpreted as bn, coy and tank numbers, or coy and tank numbers, but the true significance of these markings cannot be understood without some official comment from the Soviet Union. **Figs 8** and **9** are particularly interesting in that they are a rare example of consecutive numbering, and here at least the top figure must be the tank number within coy and bn. **Figs 20** and **21** show that at least some softskins also carried this system of tactical markings.

Some tanks also bore tactical numbering without any geometrical surround, ie, 52-06 (T-34/76D); and 58-1, 58-2, 58-3, 58-4 (Stuarts in northern Caucasus).

8   Call signs
From 1942 more tanks began to have radios and large two- or three-figure call signs began to appear in white on turret sides. (Examples of single and four digit numbers do occur, but are rare.) Some examples occur of these numbers preceding or following some of the tactical markings illustrated in **Plate XXVII: Fig 1** was preceded by 20, **Fig 6** by 240, **Fig 17** by 262, **Fig 12** by 476, and **Fig 19** was followed by 225.

Call signs became more common in 1943, as the number of radios available increased, and by 1944 were painted on the turrets, and on occasions repeated on the glacis, of almost all AFVs. By this date the geometrical tactical signs were no longer used, and the call signs appeared either on their own or together with a formation sign.

Plate XXVII (opposite): USSR tactical markings.
1 T-34/76D Stalingrad. **2** T-34/76. **4** KV1. **6** T-34. This was followed by a call sign. **7** SU100. **8** and **9** OT-133 Light flame-throwing tanks after battle of Kiev. **12** Painted in black on BA-10s and preceded by a call sign. **16** 1202nd SP Arty Regt vehicle. **20** Right rear of Studebaker lorry towing a field gun. **21** Left rear of lorry with enclosed body, repeated on right side of body behind cab. **22** Right rear of 2½-ton lorry with rocket launcher. **23** T-60. **24** T-60. **Figs 3, 5, 10, 11, 13, 14, 15, 17, 18, 19, 25, 26,** no information available.

9   Vehicle names
Slogans rather than names were used on the vehicles of the Soviet Army, and were usually of a patriotic nature. Such slogans were mostly painted on the vehicles in the front line, usually by hand by the crew members, although stencils were sometimes used, and most frequently appeared as a result of indoctrination campaigns promoted by the units' political commissars. Some examples of such slogans are given in **Plate XXVIII Figs 1-8**. The slogans normally appeared on the turret sides of AFVs, although on rare occasions they were painted on the glacis or turret rear. Rare examples of such slogans on lorries are painted on the cab doors.

Exceptions to the politically inspired type of slogan were the commemorative and presentation inscriptions, which were normally applied at the factory by stencil. Some commemorative inscriptions are listed in **Plate XXVIII Figs 9-13**. The 3A CCCP slogan was painted on tanks manned by fanatical Komsomol young men and Army School cadets. Three presentation inscriptions are shown in **Figs 14-16** on the same plate. This type of slogan was painted on all vehicles within a unit (sometimes amounting to a whole coy) which had been purchased for the State by unions, collectives, etc.

Although slogans were popular, it should not be thought that *all* AFVs carried them, and in fact only a minority of AFVs bore such slogans and inscriptions.

Plate XXVIII (below): USSR slogans.

1 For the Homeland (or Fatherland). **2** Death to the Occupiers. **3** The enemy is to be smashed. **4** To Berlin. **5** Long live the Soviet Union. **6** Forward to Victory. **7** Death to the Fascists. **8** Death to the German invaders. **9** For Stalin. **10** For Lenin. **11** For the USSR. **12** Suvorov. **13** Shchortz (a Civil War general). **14** The Kolkhoz (Collective Farmers) member of Moscow, actual Kolkhoz unidentified. Painted in red (or possibly

in black) on white KV1-M43s in 1943. **15** Chelyabinsk Kolkhoz 1943. **16** Khabarovski Youth Group; painted in black on white tanks.

10 Vehicle serial numbers

All vehicles were officially allocated a serial number. On softskin vehicles these numbers were painted in black on an oblong white panel, carried on both cab doors and repeated on a larger panel on the vehicle's rear, although sometimes it was painted in white directly on to the tailboard. The number consisted of a prefix of a letter, a letter and a digit, or possibly in some cases two numbers or two digits (most photographs containing this information are extremely fuzzy), followed by two two-digit number groups separated by a hyphen, for example: 8-30-86 (on a GAZ tanker lorry); H-96-54 (on 2½-ton rocket-launcher lorry); Л1-76 (on a lorry in the Ukraine, 1943); 52-53-32 (on a lorry during the winter of 1941-2); Л4-82-81 (on a Studebaker lorry towing a field gun).

On tanks these numbers were stencilled in white in the centre of the hull rear, but examples of such numbers actually painted on tanks are rare.

UK and USA vehicles retained the serial numbers painted on in their country of origin, at least until repainting occurred. The numerous civilian vehicles which were impressed for military service retained the civilian system of serial numbers, which is still in use today and consisted of a town prefix followed by two-digit numbers, for example, MOK 34-82, which indicates a vehicle originating from Moscow.

Plate XXVIII: USSR slogans.

1 **ЗА Родину!**

2 **СМЕРТЬ ОКУЛАНТАМ**

3 **ВРАГ БУДЕТ РАЗЕИТЬ**

4 **До Берлина**

5 **Да здравствует Советский Союз**

6 **Вперед к лобеде**

7 **Смерть фашистам**

8 **Смерть неметским захватчикам**

9 **ЗАСТАЛИНА!** or **ЗАСТАЛИНА!**

10 **ЗАЛЕНИНА**

11 **ЗА СССР**

12 **СЧВОРОВ**

13 **ШЧОРЦ**

14 **МОСКОВСКИИ КОЛХОЗНИК**

15 **ЧЕЛЯБИНСКИИ КОЛХОЗНИК**

16 **ХАБАРОВСКИИ КОМСОМОЛЕЧ**

---

11 Bridge classification numbers

No information.

12 Shipping and rail loading marks

Not applicable, except that tanks supplied by the UK often continued to carry their white stencilled shipping marks until repainted. See British section 12.

13 Ambulance markings

No information, except the occasional sighting during the first two years of the war of small *white* crosses stuck or painted on the right hand side of windscreens.

14 Other markings

Towing vehicles carried a yellow triangle on the left hand side of the tailboard. For presentation insignia see section 9.

The Axis Powers

Germany
1 National identification marks

For the invasion of Poland, the OKW ordered that all AFVs should be marked with a solid white cross or Balkenkreuz, **(Plate XXIX Fig 1)** in a prominent position to allow for easy identification by friendly forces. This cross was normally painted on hull front and both sides, and on hull or turret rear. The size depended to some extent on the type of vehicle and space available, but 10 in (25.4 cm) high was a common size for PzKpfw IIIs and IVs, and about 8 in (20.3 cm) high for PzKpfw Is and IIs. Occasionally the cross was not painted on the vehicles, but cut out of thin metal sheet and applied to vehicles' sides and radiators, particularly on armoured cars and half-tracks. Softskin vehicles did not officially carry the national symbol at this date.

It was soon found during the campaign that the solid white cross was too conspicuous and served as an aiming point for enemy gunners. During the course of the campaign, therefore, AFV crews usually daubed the cross with mud to make it less conspicuous, or covered it completely. Some crews used the dark yellow paint supplied for other markings to paint out the centre of the cross, so that only a white outline remained visible at a distance; others repainted the entire cross in yellow.

After the Polish campaign the number of Pz divs was doubled and the AFVs manufactured and passing into service during the Phoney War were marked with a new form of cross, an outline only **(Plate XXIX Fig 2)** which allowed the dark grey finish of the AFVs to show in between. This cross was not applied to the front of AFVs and on occasion was even omitted from vehicle sides: it was always displayed on the turret rear, where it was of prime importance for the supporting Inf.

However, a number of variants of the cross now began to appear. Those vehicles which had seen service in Poland did not usually erase their original white crosses and replace them with the outline version, but simply painted out their centres to leave the outlines, sometimes using dunkel grau paint, but more often using black paint, to create the cross illustrated in **Fig 3**. The width of the arms of this superimposed cross varied greatly, and on rare occasions only the horizontal arms were applied. Sometimes a black edging was also applied to the white cross, as **Fig 4**.

There were also many captured AFVs now in the German service, or SP guns on foreign chassis, and, in order to make sure these were recognised as friendly, larger versions of the national cross were painted on them, appearing on both sides of the hull, and on hull front and rear.

Therefore, for the invasions of Norway, Holland and France, there were a number of national identification symbols in use, even rare examples of the Balkenkreuz in Norway—and again for the invasion of the USSR in 1941.

The opening of the North African campaign in February 1941, where all vehicles were painted an overall dunkel gelb, led to the official introduction of the form of cross illustrated by **Fig 3**. This cross was only official for North Africa, so a variety of crosses continued to appear elsewhere—and indeed in Africa itself. However, in Europe the emphasis shifted more and more to the other official type **(Plate XXIX Fig 2)** as new vehicles were issued and old ones went in for repair, respraying and re-marking.

In February 1943 the overall dunkel gelb colour became official for all vehicles and the black and white cross **(Fig 3)** therefore became the only official national identification symbol in all theatres.

In 1944-5, as camouflage paint was changed,

Zimmerit applied, and AFV losses increased, many crews had to paint their vehicles' markings by hand. They almost always maintained the use of the national identification symbol, using either the white outline or black cross edged white designs, though in the case of the latter the width of the arms of the black cross again varied greatly.

Roumania was forced into the Axis alliance in 1940 and contributed 12 divs to the Eastern Front: Roumanian AFVs in that theatre carried a simplified version of the national cross on hull sides: see **Plate XXIX Fig 5**.

Finland 'loaned' Germany ten divs for the Eastern Front, and in that theatre Finnish AFVs —most of which were of Soviet origin—carried the Finnish hakaristi (**Plate XXIX Fig 6**) on turret sides and rear, on the glacis, and occasionally on the hull rear of some AFV types. The hakaristi was painted in dark blue or black and 'blocked' with white. The white blocking was normally to the right of the symbol as you view it, and varied in width. Later in the war the arms of the hakaristi were shortened to distinguish it from the Nazi swastika (**Plate XXIX Fig 7**). In 1945 the hakaristi was abandoned, and a 'roundel' was used in its place; (**Plate XXIX Fig 8**). This had a white outer circle and a blue inner disc, with the vehicle colour showing between the two.

Plate XXIX (below): German national identification marks.
Figs 1-4 forms of German cross. **5** Roumanian symbol. **6** and **7** Finnish symbols. **8** Finnish symbol, 1945. **9** Roumanian aerial recognition symbol.

2 Aerial recognition symbols
For the Polish campaign the Balkenkreuz was used on turret tops or engine decks, and was still in use in the 1940 campaigns, although it was no longer universal, for broad white bands or rectangles, black swastikas on white circles, or plain white swastikas were now being painted on horizontal surfaces, including the bonnets or cab roofs of softskins. The swastikas seem to have been mostly hand painted as an impromptu aerial recognition symbol.

From 1941 onwards the Nazi national flag, a black swastika on a white disc on a rectangular red field, was draped or tied over a horizontal surface as an aerial recognition symbol, usually on the bonnets of softskins and half-tracks, on the engine decks of AFVs. The flag was very effective for this purpose and had the advantage of being easy to remove if the enemy at any time achieved local air superiority.

In 1943-5, as the Allies gained aerial supremacy in the various theatres, the use of all aerial recognition symbols declined, and such symbols were rarely used from mid-1944 onwards, except the occasional use of Allied symbols to fool enemy aircraft.

Roumanian AFVs carried a large, simplified version of the national cross on their engine decks: see **Plate XXIX Fig 9**. This was yellow, edged white, and bore in the centre a blue circle, edged at both inner and outer edges with white. The Finnish hakaristi was occasionally painted on the hatches of turrets of Finnish AFVs, but

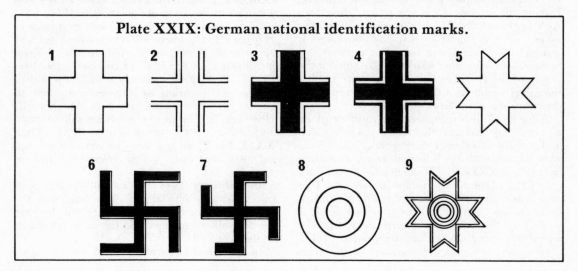

Plate XXIX: German national identification marks.

these may not have been intended as aerial recognition symbols, being visible from the ground when the hatches were open.

3 Rank, signal and other flags

Official designs for standards and pennants existed at the beginning of the war for all commands within the Wehrmacht. According to the Bundesarchiv records, all were intended to be painted in black and white only, directly on to the front left wing of vehicles. The standards and pennants are illustrated in **Plate XXX Figs 1-16**, and it can be seen that they could, in fact, only be shown correctly by painting them on vehicles, it being impossible to convert **Figs 4, 5, 9, 10** and **11** into actual flags or even flags painted on metal plates.

However, this was a far from convenient system, restricting the movement of a cmdr from one vehicle to another, and by January 1941 a new system was in use. This continued to use the original system, but added colour and borders to the flags. The flags could now be painted on to thin sheet metal plates and 'flown' from metal rods attached to the front left of vehicles, with a duplicate of the plate at the rear beside the serial number plate. When cmdrs were not in the vehicles, their command plates could now be covered by canvas envelopes with press studs to hold them in position, and should they need to change vehicles, it was relatively simple to shift these metal plates to other vehicles.

Under the new system a red border was used on the flags of Wehrmacht cmdr and Army Group cmdrs, that of the latter sometimes having the border halved, the inner half being red, the outer white. The Army cmdrs' flags now had a white border. Corps cmdrs' flags now had a red lower triangle instead of a black one, and div pennants had black/white/red bars instead of black/white/black. In addition, the pennants for divs and below now had the white section in the Waffenfarbe (arm of service colour) to identify the type of unit within the div, etc. A standard for Pz Army Group cmdr was introduced in early 1941; a square divided by two diagonal lines, the top and bottom triangles thus formed being black, the side triangles red, the whole surrounded by a white border.

From about the same date (January 1941) div formation signs and/or numbers began to be painted on the central section of the div pennants, while bn pennants carried the bn number, in Roman numerals for bns within a regt, and in Arabic numerals for independent bns. From about October 1943 some regt and bn

level flags also carried a tactical emblem to identify the type of unit: see section 7 for these emblems.

The personal rank flags for officers of General rank were 20 cm deep by 30 cm long, and were of a grey-green colour with white border and Nazi insignia: see **Plate XXX Fig 17**. Two new patterns (**Figs 18** and **19**) were introduced in April 1941, a 30 cm square standard for Field Marshals, and a new pennant for Generals. The old pennants remained in use for officials and field grade officers. The Marshal's standard was probably only ever used in textile form, of grey-green cloth, heavily embroidered with crossed batons and the Nazi eagle. The hafts of the batons were red, the crosses on them black edged silver, the remainder of the embroidery in gold except the heads of the batons, which were edged in silver. If the standard was ever painted on a metal plate, white and yellow paints would probably have been used. The General's pennant also had gold insignia, with a more elaborate border than before, and was normally used in textile form, attached to a metal rod.

These rank standards and pennants were carried on the right front of vehicles, and were only flown when the officer was in the vehicle. It was usual for both personal and command flags to be used on the one vehicle.

The national flag was also flown from vehicles on rare occasions, though it is not known if it was used to denote any command vehicle. Regt flags also appeared on rare occasions on combat vehicles, but this is a whole new subject, and readers are referred to B.L. Davis's excellent book, *Flags & Standards of the Third Reich*.

Waffen-SS field units used the Wehrmacht car pennant system, with the single addition of a different flag for Territorial Cmdr (**Plate XXX Fig 7**). However, a number of unofficial pennants were also used by special units, such as SS-Kampfgruppen: some of these consisted simply of the group cmdr's name in white on a red or black rectangular field. Other SS units employed a totally different system, but as most of these were not combat units they fall outside the scope of this book. However, a small selection of the most appropriate pennants and standards has been illustrated in **Plate XXXI**.

The Fallschirm-PanzerKorps utilised the Wehrmacht design of standard but with the flying eagle and swastika of the Luftwaffe in gold in the centre. Other Fallschirmjäger formations also used the Wehrmacht car pennant system, with the addition of the Luftwaffe emblem in gold for div and bde cmdrs, in white for regt and

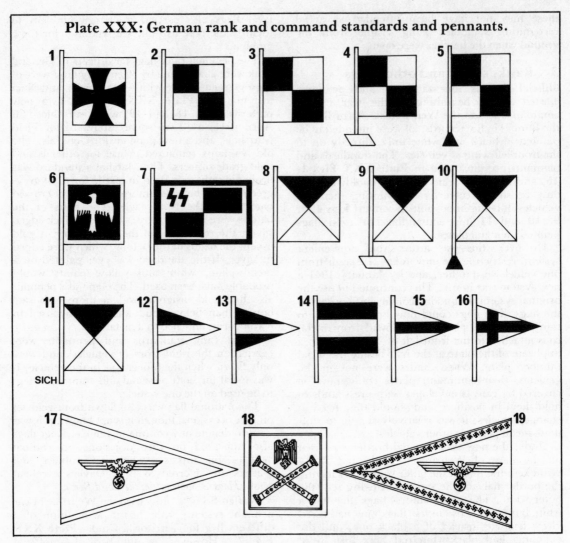

Plate XXX: German rank and command standards and pennants.

bn cmdrs. Cmdrs of independent coys used an all-white pennant with a black outline of the Luftwaffe eagle and swastika. 1HG or 2HG was carried in the canton of the regt standards of the Grenadier Regts Hermann Göring, with Roman numerals added to indicate bn, for example, II/2HG. The type of regt or bn was indicated by Waffenfarbe as in the Wehrmacht. Where there was only a single regt (as Jager-Regt Hermann Göring) or bn (as Pz-Pionier-Bn Hermann Göring), then only the initials HG were carried.

Signal flags were not flown on Wehrmacht vehicles, a semaphore system being used instead. As the implements used for this system were not attached to the vehicle, the system falls outside the scope of this book.

Plate XXX (above): German rank and command standards and pennants.

1 Oberkommando des Heeres. **2** Heeresgruppen kommando. **3** Armeeoberkommando. **4** Panzer-Armeeoberkommando. **5** Gebirgs-Armeeoberkommando. **6** Militärbefehlshaber (Territorial cmdr). **7** Befehlshaber der Waffen-SS (Waffen-SS Territorial cmdr). **8** Generalkommando Armee Korps. (Rommel used such a standard for the Afrika Korps, with the word AFRIKA in black across the lower (red) triangle.) On occasions rectangular corps standards of the same design were used. **9** Generalkommando eines Panzerkorps. **10** Generalkommando eines Gebirgskorps. **11** Kommandierender general der

Sicherungstruppen und Befehlshaber im Heeresgebiet (commanding general Security Troops and commanding officer Army District). **12** Kommando einer division. **13** Brigade cmdr. **14** Regt cmdr. **15** Bn cmdr, for bn within regt. **16** Cmdr of indep bn. **17** General's pennant to April 1941. **18** General's pennant from April 1941. **19** Field Marshal's standard from April 1941.

Plate XXXI (below): German standards and pennants, Waffen-SS.

1 SS District cmdr: 35 by 20 cm, name of district in Gothic script below eagle. **2** SS Sub-district cmdr, 35 by 20 cm. **3** SS Regt (34th) cmdr, 25 cm square. Cav regt cmdrs had crossed lances to each side of regt number. **4** SS Bn cmdr, 25 by 40 cm. Example illustrated is 1st Bn (Sturmbann) of 1st Regt (Standarte). Engineer Bn cmdrs used the same design with crossed spade and pick to left of swastika, and with pi in Gothic script to right. **5** All SS vehicles, 25 by 40 cm.

4   Formation signs

At the outbreak of war in 1939 only some of the Army's divs had formation signs, apparently adopted unofficially. Amongst these divs were the five Pz divs. The use of these formation signs for identifying vehicles within formations, yet keeping the identity of that formation secret from the enemy, proved so successful in the Polish campaign that the signs were adopted on a much

wider scale for the campaigns of 1940 and were now officially approved by the OKW. Some divs which had had signs in 1939 now adopted new signs for security reasons, but others kept their original designs. There were now ten Pz divs and in 1940 these mostly used completely new signs, and for the first time a definite pattern emerged: see **Plate XXXV** for the 1940 signs of 5, 6 and 7 Pz Divs (an inverted Y with 1, 2 and 3 dots respectively) and 8, 9 and 10 Pz Divs (a Y with 1, 2 and 3 dots respectively).

In the late summer and autumn of 1940 the Pz divs were re-organised and as a result increased to 20 in number. For the invasion of the USSR the OKW devised a completely new series of formation signs for these divs (see **Plates XXXV** and **XXXVI**). However, some of the original Pz divs preferred to retain their old signs, or use old and new together, so no hard lines may be drawn as to precisely which sign was used and when. At this same date, OKW had ordered that for the invasion of the USSR *all* Army vehicles must carry a formation sign, but the choice of sign was for the most part left to the discretion of the div cmdrs.

It was intended that these signs be used just for the invasion of the USSR, but in fact most remained in use for the remainder of the war, the only changes being when divs were destroyed and new divs of the same number reformed; mostly in 1943 after the appalling losses at Stalingrad and in Tunisia; and occasionally when div cmdrs were changed and they or their men chose a new sign. Thus a number of unofficial signs tended to appear, and there was

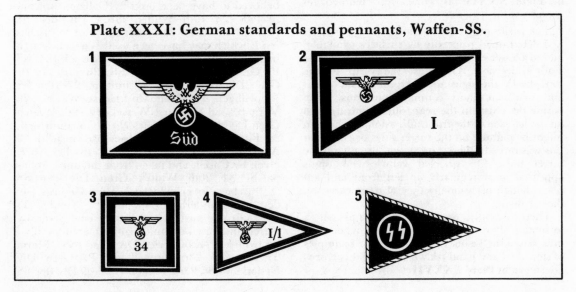

Plate XXXI: German standards and pennants, Waffen-SS.

inevitably a certain amount of duplication of signs, which the OKW proved unable to control. The reason was that formations rapidly identified with their signs, and the benefit to morale and the preservation of tradition (many signs were linked to the place of origin or history of a formation) far outweighed any confusion which might possibly arise.

Most signs, particularly in the Pz divs, were painted in deep yellow in the early years, either solid or in outline. In North Africa, and when overall dunkel gelb was introduced as the basic camouflage colour for all theatres in February 1943, the markings were changed to white, again either solid or in outline. These signs were often outlined in black or painted on black fields, particularly in the USSR where snow camouflage was used extensively.

Some signs employed coloured paints, and details of the colours are listed in the captions where known. (15th Pz Div in North Africa specified red for its sign, but black and white were also used.) However, no colour details are known for many of the Inf signs: it is possible that many coloured signs were in any case reduced to stylised versions in white for convenience when painted on vehicles.

The signs of the SS divs were always in white, unless camouflage dictated otherwise. On occasions they were surrounded by the outline of a shield, of which there were four shapes, denoting the type of div, Pz, Pz-Grenadier, Mountain and Cav, and Grenadier, ie, Inf. The arm patches of Foreign Legions have been given in **Plate XXXIV** as some were painted on vehicles of the legions.

The positioning of formation signs on vehicles was determined primarily by surfaces available, and to a lesser extent by the unit and even vehicle cmdr's decision. On most tanks up to the PzKpfw IV the signs appeared on the hull front and rear, the most common positions being beside the cross on the rear (often central), and on the left side of the front. Occasionally the sign might be painted on the turret sides or rear, but this was rare. In these cases it was usually on the turret bins. On wheeled vehicles the signs appeared most regularly on left front and left rear, though occasionally they also appeared on the cab doors.

There is only one known example of a formation sign used for a formation higher than div, that of the Deutsches Afrikakorps. Examples of stencilled and hand-drawn signs for this Korps are shown in **Plate XXXVII**.

Plate XXXII (opposite): German formation signs, Waffen-SS.

1 1st SS Pz Div Leibstandarte Adolf Hitler. The div was motorised Infantry from 1939 to 1941, and as such had the plain shield outline shown in **Fig 25, Plate XXXIII**. It became a Pz Div for the invasion of the USSR. Vehicles of the SS Pz Korps Leibstandarte carried the sign illustrated but with 2 oak leaves below the shield outline. **2** 2nd SS Pz Div Das Reich. **3** Variant used by Das Reich until 1944. **4** 3rd SS Pz Div Totenkopf. **5** 4th SS-Pollizei Pz-Gren Div. **6** Variant used by Polizei Pz-Gren Div until 1944: it was bright green. **7** 5th SS Pz-Gren Div Wiking. **8** 6th SS Gebirgs Div Nord. **9** Variant used by Nord, usually with rectangular background. **10** 7th Freiwilligen Gebirgs Div Prinz Eugen: this sign sometimes appeared with a circle round it instead of a shield outline. **11** 8th SS Kavallerie Div Florian Geyer: the sword often appeared on its own as a simplified marking. **12** 9th SS Pz Div Hohenstaufen: sometimes painted in light blue with the sword reversed, on a yellow shield with flat top, straight sides, and two straight bottom edges meeting in a sharp point. **13** Variant used by Hohenstaufen after Arnhem, in red. **14** 10th SS Pz Div Frundsberg. **15** Variant used by Frundsberg, white on yellow rhomboid field. **16** 11th SS Freiwilligen Pz-Gren Div Nordland. **17** Variant used by Nordland. **18** 12th SS Pz Div Hitler Jugend: crossed oakleaves were added below during the 1943-4 period. **19** 13th Waffen Gebirgs Div der SS Handschar (Kroatisches No 1). **20** Variant used by Handschar. **21** 14th Waffen Gren Div der SS Galizien. **22** Variant believed to have been used by Galizien: unconfirmed. **23** 15th Waffen Gren Div der SS (Lettisches No 1). **24** Collar patch of Lettisches No 1, which may have been used as a vehicle sign instead of that illustrated in **Fig 23. 25** 16th SS Pz Gren Div Reichsführer SS. **26** 17th SS Pz Gren Div Götz von Berlichingen. **27** 18th SS Freiwilligen Pz Gren Div Horst Wessel. **28** Variant used by Horst Wessel. **29** 19th Waffen Gren Div de SS (Lettisches No 2): unconfirmed, see **Fig 24** which may have been used instead. **30** Alternative vehicle marking for Lettisches No 2, given by Carell, and taken from the unit's collar patch. **31** 20th Waffen Gren Div der SS (Estnisches No 1). **32** 21st Waffen Gebirgs Div der SS Skanderbeg (Albanisches No 1). **33** Unconfirmed variant for Skanderbeg, given by Carell and based on unit's collar patch. **34** 22nd Freiwilligen Kavallerie Div der SS Maria Theresa. **35** 23rd Freiwilligen Pz Gren Div Nederland. **36** 23rd Waffen Gebirgs Div der SS

Plate XXXII: German formation signs, Waffen-SS.

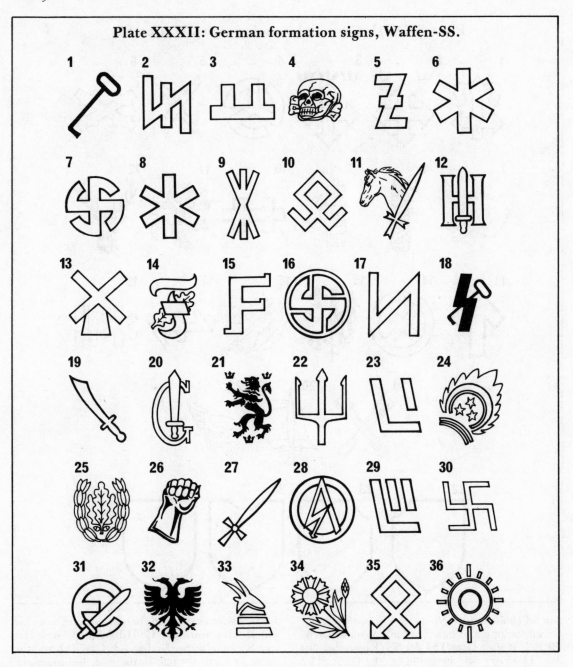

Kama (Kroatisches No 2).

Plate XXXIII (overleaf): German formation signs, Waffen-SS.

1 24th Waffen Gebirgs (Karstjäger) Div der SS.
2 25th Waffen Gren Div der SS Hunyadi (Ungarisches No 1): a large H, from the unit's collar patch, is also shown by Carell. **3** 26th Waffen Gren Div der SS (Ungarisches No 2). **4** 27th SS Freiwilligen Gren Div Langemarck. **5** 28th SS Freiwilligen Pz-Gren Div Wallonie. **6** Variant used by Wallonie and based on cross raguly of Burgundy. **7** 29th Waffen Gren Div der SS (Russisches No 1). **8** 29th Waffen Gren Div

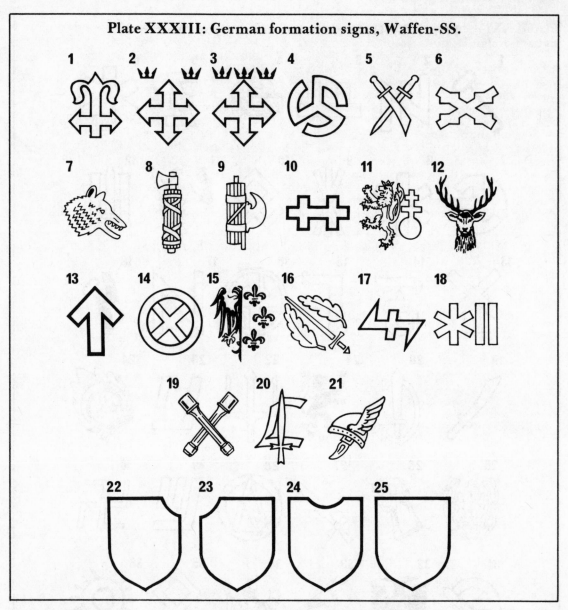

Plate XXXIII: German formation signs, Waffen-SS.

der SS (Italienisches No 1). **9** Variant given by Carell for 29th and based on unit's collar patch. **10** 30th Waffen Gren Div der SS (Russisches No 2). **11** 31st SS Freiwilligen Pz-Gren Div Böhman-Mähren. Also referred to as 31st SS Freiwilligen Gren Div. **12** Variant used by 31st Div. **13** 32nd SS Pz-Gren Div 30 Januar. **14** 33rd Waffen Kavallerie Div der SS (Ungarisches No 4): unconfirmed, based on unit's collar patch. **15** 33rd Waffen Gren Div Charlemagne (Französisches No 1). **16** Variant given by Carell

for Charlemagne and based on unit's collar patch. Unconfirmed. **17** 34th Waffen Gren Div der SS Landstorm Nederland: Carell shows the same emblem for late in the war, but gives the emblem turned into a vertical position for earlier. **18** 35th SS Polizei Gren Div. **19** 36th SS Sturm-Div Dirlewanger. **20** 37th Waffen Kavallerie Div Lützow. **21** 38th SS Pz-Gren Div Nibelungen. **22-25**, shield outlines for Pz, Pz-Gren, Gebirgs and Kavallerie, and Gren divisions respectively.

Plate XXXIV (below): German formation signs; Foreign Legions.

1 Don Cossacks of Cossack Liberation Armies: yellow shield outline and top, light blue over red shield. This shield shape was used for Wehrmacht badges. **2** Don Cossacks, with Waffen SS shield shape: green shield outline and top, red top and bottom sections to shield, other sections light blue. **3** Kuban Cossacks, Wehrmacht pattern: yellow lettering, red top and bottom sections to shield, other sections yellow. **4** Kuban Cossacks, Waffen SS pattern: green shield outline and top, red top and bottom sections, others navy bluc. **5** Terek Cossacks,

Wehrmacht pattern: green over red shield. **6** Terek Cossacks, Waffen SS pattern: green shield outline and top, top and bottom sections light blue, others navy blue. **7** Kaminsky Legion (later 29th Waffen Div): green shield with gold lettering. **8** Weissruthenien Legion (later 30th Waffen Gren Div): red top and edging to shield, also central 'pale', gold lettering and cross. **9** Slowakei Legion: red shield, white top, cross and edging, light blue lettering and 'hills'. **10** Latvian Legion (later 15th and 19th Waffen Gren Divs): red shield, gold lettering. **11** Croatian Legion: white and red checkered shield. **12** Bulgarian Legion: white/green/red shield. **13** Lithuanian Legion: red shield, grey

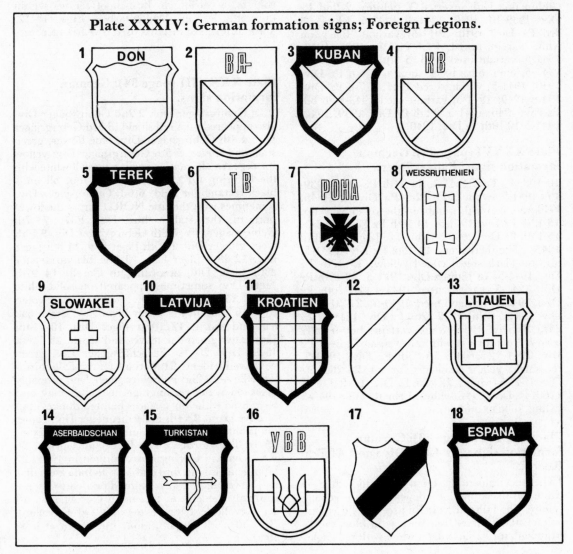

Plate XXXIV: German formation signs; Foreign Legions.

emblem, gold lettering, green top and edging. **14** Azerbaidzhan Legion: red lettering, light blue/red/light green field. **15** Turkistan Legion (later 162nd Inf Div): red over blue field. **16** Ukrainian Legion: green top and edging to shield, yellow over light blue field. **17** Estonian Legion: light blue/black/white shield. **18** Spanish Legion (later 250th Inf Div): red/yellow/red field.

Plate XXXV (opposite): German formation signs; Panzer Divs.

All signs were yellow in the 1939-42 period unless otherwise stated. **1** 1st Pz Div: 1940; 1941-5, also appearing in France in 1940; 1940-5 introduced for Operation Citadel and used later in conjunction with inverted Y (white). **2** 2nd Pz Div: 1939-40; 1940; 1941-3; 1943-5 (white). **3** 3rd Pz Div: 1940; 1941-5; variant, black on white; variant in red. **4** 4th Pz Div: 1939; 1940; 1941-5; variant used 1943. **5** 5th Pz Div: 1940; 1941-5, often on a black square. **6** 6th Pz Div: 1940; 1941-5; variant used 1941. **7** 7th Pz Div: 1940; 1940; 1941-5; variant used 1943-4. **8** 8th Pz Div: 1940; 1941-5. **9** 9th Pz Div: 1939; 1940; 1941-5. **10** 10th Pz Div: 1940.

Plate XXXVI (page 82): German formation signs; Panzer Divs.

10 10th Pz Div: 1941-3. **11** 11th Pz Div: 1939-45; 1941-5 (white). **12** 12th Pz Div: 1939-45: Feldgrau shows this emblem the other way up. **13** 13th Pz Div: 1941-5. **14** 14th Pz Div: 1941-5. **15** 15th Pz Div: 1940-5 (white, red or black until 1943, white thereafter). **16** 16th Pz Div: 1941-5, also on black shield edged yellow. **17** 17th Pz Div: 1941-5. **18** 18th Pz Div: 1941-5. **19** 19th Pz Div: 1941-5; variant used 1943-4. **20** 20th Pz Div: 1941-5; variant used 1943-5. **21** 21st Pz Div: 1941-5 (white). **22** 22nd Pz Div: 1941-3. **23** 23rd Pz Div: 1941; white variant, but usually used in conjunction with other sign. **24** 24th Pz Div: 1941-5; variant. **25** 25th Pz Div: 1943-5, red shield, yellow emblems; variant. **26** 26th Pz Div: 1943-5 (white). **27** 27th Pz Div: 1942-3. **116** 116th Pz Div: 1944 (white). Lehr Pz Div: 1943-5 (white, solid or outline).

Plate XXXVII (page 83): German formation signs; Pz-Gren Divs and Afrika Korps.

1 Grossdeutschland Pz-Gren Div: solid white or white or black outline, depending on vehicle colour. The FührerEscort Bn used a solid yellow helmet, the Führer-Gren Bn a solid blue one. **2** Brandenburg Pz-Gren Div: white with red eagle,

yellow beak and claws. **3** 3rd Pz-Gren Div. **4** 10th Pz-Gren Div: a large F in solid yellow was used until 1943: a white key symbol, as shown, thereafter. Sometimes the key was surrounded by a shield outline. **5** 14th Pz-Gren Div. For 16th Pz-Gren Div see 116th Pz Div, formed from the 16th and retaining the same greyhound emblem. **6** 18th Pz-Gren Div. **7** 20th Pz-Gren Div: yellow. **8** Variant for 20th. **9** 22nd (Luftlande) Pz-Gren Div: 4 white and 3 red vertical bars with colours reversed in the squares. **10** 25th Pz-Gren Div. **11** 29th Pz-Gren Div. **12** 60th Pz-Gren Div (Feldherrnhalle): two yellow crosses; the shield was sometimes omitted. **13** 90th Pz-Gren Div: white map of Sardinia with bayonet of various colours, according to branch of service within division, ie, in Waffenfarbe. **Figs 14-17**. Various forms of insignia used by Afrika Korps.

Plate XXXVIII (page 84): German formation signs.

1 1st Gebirgsjäger Div. **2** 2nd Gebirgsjäger Div: also appeared on a red shield. **3** 3rd Gebirgsjäger Div. **4** 4th Gebirgsjäger Div: blue flower, green stalk and leaves. **5** 5th Gebirgsjäger Div: yellow 'peaks'. An alternative version was all white with the lettering GEMSE across the top, all on a black rectangular field. **6** 6th Gebirgsjäger Div: sometimes with the title NORD across the lower part of the stalk, thus NO RD. **7** 7th Gebirgsjäger Div. **8** 8th Gebirgsjäger Div. **9** 10th Gebirgsjäger Div. **10** 5th Jäger Div. **11** 8th Jäger Div. **12** 28th Jäger Div. **13** Possible variant for 28th Jäger Div, according to Carell. **14** 97th Jäger Div: sometimes appeared on solid white shield. **15** 100th Jäger Div: yellow S over green tree. **16** Variant for 100th Jäger Div: green oak leaf and acorn. **17** 101st Jäger Div. **18** 114th Jäger Div: green oak leaves and acorn. **19** 118th Jäger Div. **20** 1st Fallschirmjäger Div: green devil, red trident. **21** Variant for 1st Fallschirmjäger Div. **22** 2nd Fallschirmjäger Div: probably black on white rectangular field, but may also have used white on surfaces painted dunkel grau or olive grun. **23** 4th Fallschirmjäger Div: comet tail is blue/red/blue. **24** Luftwaffen Felddivision. **25** 1st Fallschirm-Pz Div Hermann Göring. **26** Regt General Göring: discontinued in 1941. **27** Unofficial Viking ship emblem, to indicate a unit had served in Norway, painted on doors of some company vehicles in Hermann Göring Div. **28** 1st Kavallerie Div: yellow. **29** 3rd Kavallerie Div. **30** Todt Organisation, used from at least 1940.

Plate XXXV: German formation signs; Panzer Divs.

Plate XXXVI: German formation signs; Panzer Divs.

Lehr

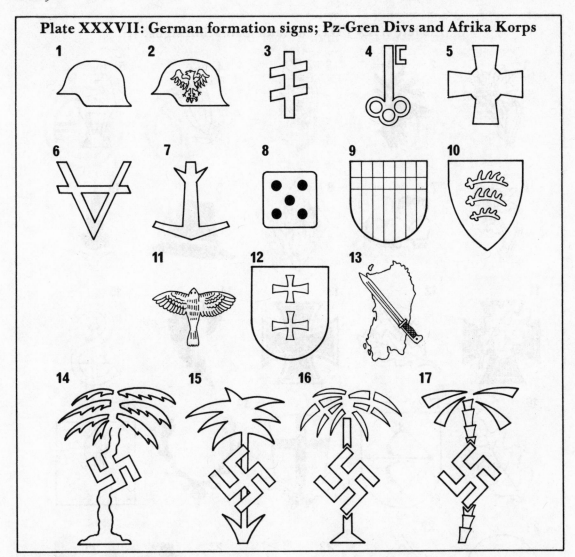

Plate XXXVII: German formation signs; Pz-Gren Divs and Afrika Korps

Plate XXXIX (page 85): German formation signs; Inf Divs.

1 1st Inf Div. **2** 6th Inf Div. **3** 7th Inf Div: as shown by Carell, Hartmann gives a blue rectangle. **4** 9th Inf Div. **5** 11th Inf Div: sometimes shown without the shield, which is red over white. Hartmann also gives a solid blue disc within a white square. **6** 12th Inf Div. **7** 12th Inf Div: variant used until 1943; shield is red/blue/yellow over white bar. **8** 14th Inf Div. **9** 15th Inf Div. **10** 16th Inf Div. **11** 17th Inf Div. **12** 18th Inf Div. **13** 21st Inf Div; Hartmann also gives a large red disc on a white square in use in 1943. **14** 22nd Inf Div (motorised): colours unknown but possibly red and white. **15** 24th Inf Div: also shown without the field. **16** 26th Inf Div. **17** 30th Inf Div: three red bars; sometimes shown upright. **18** 31st Inf Div. **19** 32nd Inf Div. **20** 34th Inf Div: wavy blue diagonal. **21** 35th Inf Div: yellow outline. Occasionally shown facing opposite direction, and sometimes painted in a more natural form. **22** 36th Inf Div (motorised). **23** 38th Inf Div. **24** 44th Inf Div (Reichsgren-div Hoch und Deutschmeister): red/white/red shield. **25** 44th Inf Div: new division formed after Stalingrad. **26** 45th Inf Div. **27** 46th Inf Div. **28** 48th Inf Div: blue/white; division created 1944 from 171 Reserve Div, which used the same sign. **29** 50th Inf Div. **30** 52nd Inf Div.

Plate XXXVIII: German formation signs.

1

2

3 NARVIK 19 40

4

5

6

7

8

9

10

11

12

13

14

15 S

16

17

18

19

20

21 O

22 R

23

24

25

26

27

28

29 vB

30 O T

Plate XXXIX: German formation signs; Inf Divs.

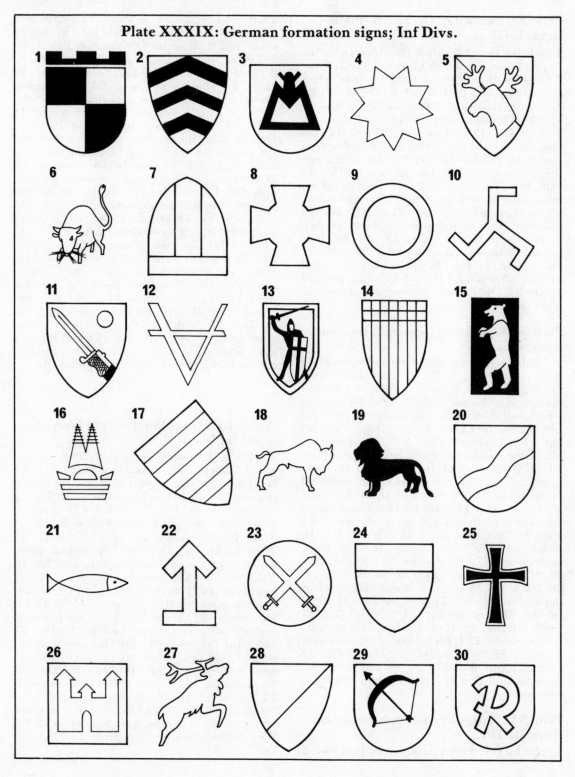

Plate XL (opposite): German formation signs; Inf Divs.

1 56th Inf Div. **2** 57th Inf Div: blue and white (arms of Bavaria). **3** 58th Inf Div. **4** 61st Inf Div. **5** 62nd Inf Div: yellow. **6** 62nd Inf Div: yellow variant used mid-1944. **7** 65th Inf Div. **8** 71st Inf Div: green clover leaf. **9** 72nd Inf Div: yellow. **10** 73rd Inf Div: white over red. **11** 75th Inf Div. **12** 76th Inf Div. **13** 78th Inf Div: 1939-42. **14** 78th (Sturm) Div: 1943-5, red mailed fist and edge of shield. **15** 79th Inf Div. **16** 81st Inf Div: sometimes appeared on red disc. **17** 83rd Inf Div. **18** 86th Inf Div. **19** 87th Inf Div: green heart. Sometimes shown as green heart with white edging only. **20** 88th Inf Div. **21** 89th Inf Div. **22** 93rd Inf Div: upper part of shield is red, remainder of sign is white. **23** 94th Inf Div: sometimes shown without the shield. **24** 95th Inf Div. **25** 96th Inf Div. **26** 98th Inf Div. **27** 102nd Inf Div. **28** 106th Inf Div. **29** 110th Inf Div. **30** 111th Inf Div: yellow. Sometimes shown on black rectangle.

Plate XLI (page 88): German formation signs; Inf Divs.

1 112th Inf Div: reddish-brown diagonal and edging, according to Carell. Hartmann shows the diagonal coming from top right and without the two white lines. **2** 121st Inf Div. **3** 122nd Inf Div: Carell gives the talon on its own. **4** 125th Inf Div. **5** 126th Inf Div. **6** 129th Inf Div. **7** 131st Inf Div. **8** 132nd Inf Div. **9** 134th Inf Div: Hartmann also gives a green heart edged white. **10** 137th Inf Div. **11** 161st Inf Div: Feldgrau shows the disc filling the centre of the shield. **12** 162nd Inf Div: red T over blue arrow. Not used after June 1944. **13** 164th Inf Div: Carell shows the same swords without letter or shield. **14** 168th Inf Div: green shield. **15** 170th Inf Div. **16** 183rd Inf Div: red triangle bearing black inverted one. **17** 197th Inf Div. **18** 198th Inf Div. **19** 205th Inf Div: red spots on white toadstool. **20** 206th Inf Div: Carell shows this emblem sloping from top left. **21** 207th Inf Div. **22** 208th Inf Div. **23** 211th Inf Div. **24** 215th Inf Div. **25** 216th Inf Div. **26** 217th Inf Div: also appears without shield. **27** 218th Inf Div: sometimes used without field. **28** 223rd Inf Div: blue shield. **29** 225th Inf Div. **30** 227th Inf Div: as shown by Feldgrau and Carell, date unknown. See also next plate.

Plate XLII (page 89): German formation signs; Inf Divs.

1 227th Inf Div: 1940-3, as shown by Feldgrau. **2** 227th Inf Div: 1943-5, as shown by Feldgrau. **3** 232nd Inf Div: blue. **4** 246th Inf Div: shield edged red. **5** 250th Inf Div (Spanish Blue Div): red/yellow/red. **6** 251st Inf Div. **7** 252nd Inf Div. **8** 253rd Inf Div. **9** 255th Inf Div: green disc. **10** 256th Inf Div: as shown by Carell. Feldgrau shows only the emblem, laid horizontally and with a short bar vertically across the centre. **11** 257th Inf Div. **12** 258th Inf Div. **13** 260th Inf Div. **14** 262nd Inf Div: blue wavy lines. **15** 263rd Inf Div. 267th Inf Div used basically the same emblem as 216th. **16** 268th Inf Div: as shown by Hartmann. Carell shows a crossbow pointing upwards. **17** 268th Inf Div: variant. 272nd Inf Div used basically the same emblem as 216th. **18** 278th Inf Div. **19** 282nd Inf Div. **20** 290th Inf Div: sometimes the sword was used on its own. **21** 291st Inf Div: green leaf, red shield edging. **22** 291st Inf Div: variant in yellow. **23** 292nd Inf Div: red/white/red emblem used from September 1943. Before this date a blue ring on a white rectangle was used. **24** 293rd Inf Div: brown bear. **25** 294th Inf Div: green. **26** 297th Inf Div. **27** 299th Inf Div: green over white, green border; used until 1943. **28** 299th Inf Div: used after 1943. Carell shows the emblem reversed. **29** 302nd Inf Div. **30** 305th Inf Div.

Page XLIII (page 90): German formation signs; Inf Divs.

1 319th Inf Div: white over red. **2** 320th Inf Div: red. **3** 320th Inf Div: variant used early 1943, red heart on white disc edged red. **4** 327th Inf Div: red eagle, yellow beak and talons. **5** 329th Inf Div. **6** 331st Inf Div. **7** 334th Inf Div: yellow arrow, red circle, green palm. **8** 335th Inf Div. **9** 338th Inf Div: white and blue diamonds. **10** 340th Inf Div. **11** 347th Inf Div: yellow. 349th Inf Div used basically same emblem as 217th. **12** 353rd Inf Div. **13** 356th Inf Div: green oak leaf and acorn. **14** 357th Inf Div. 362nd Inf Div used basically same emblem as 268th. **15** 369th Inf Div: white and red checker. 373rd Inf Div used basically the same emblem. **16** 376th Inf Div. **17** 384th Inf Div. **18** 389th Inf Div: green arrow, edge of field red. 392nd Inf Div used basically same emblem as 369th. **19** 709th Inf Div. **20** 710th Inf Div. **21** 711th Inf Div: red diamond. **22** 715th Inf Div (motorised): as given by Feldgrau and Carell. **23** 715th Inf Div: as given by Hartmann, three red roundels. **24** 715th Inf Div: variant given by Hartmann. **25** 716th Inf Div.

Plate XL: German formation signs; Inf Divs.

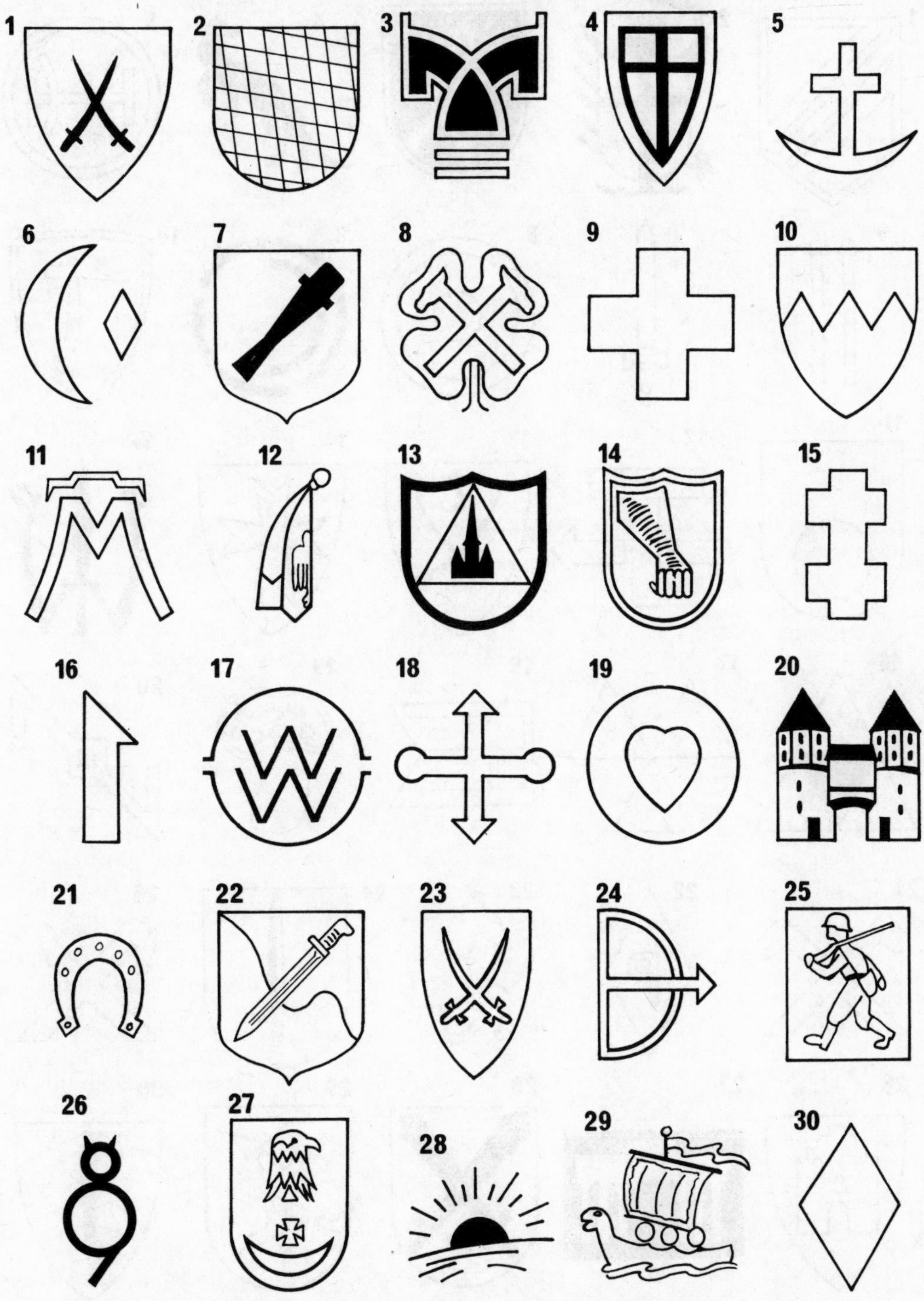

1

2

3

4

5

6

7

8

9

10

11

12

13

14

15

16

17

18

19

20

21

22

23

24

25

26

27

28

29

30

Plate XLI: German formation signs; Inf Divs.

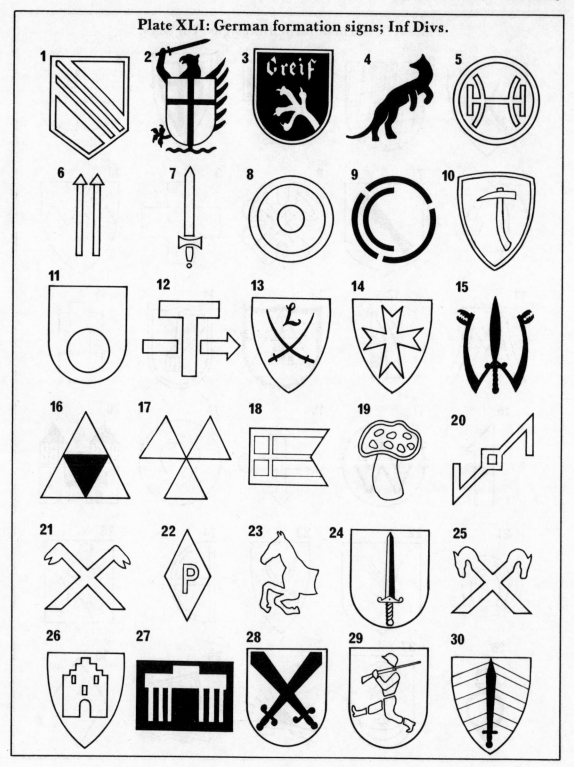

Plate XLII: German formation signs; Inf Divs.

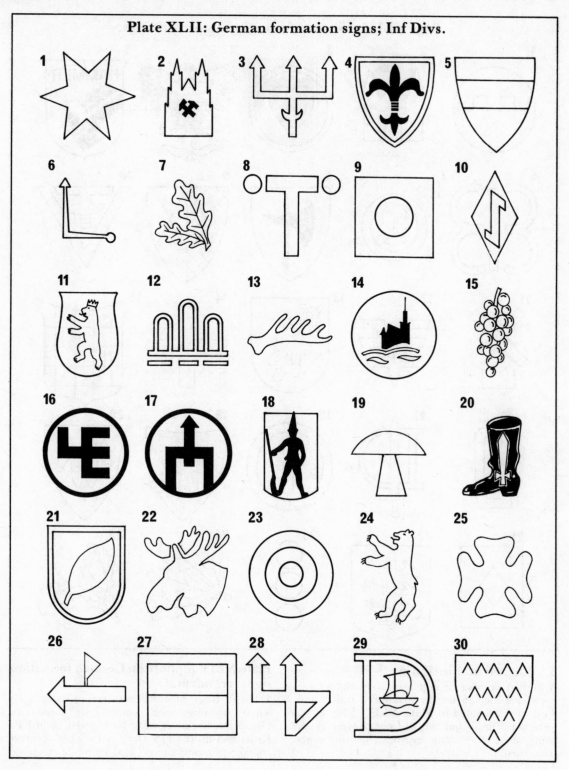

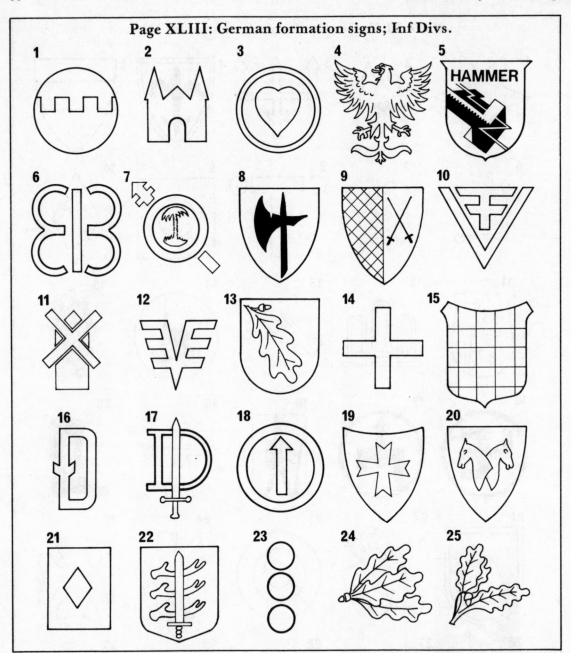

Page XLIII: German formation signs; Inf Divs.

5   Regimental insignia

A limited number of regt formation signs have been identified in use by armoured units, and these are illustrated in **Plate XLIV**. Such signs were not official, but this did not prevent them being used over long periods by the regts concerned.

Plate XLIV (opposite): German formation signs; regimental.

1 2nd Pz Regt: in white on turrets of PzKpfw IIs when training with amphibious tanks for Operation Seelöwe, near Kiel, 1940. **2** 3rd Pz Regt, 2nd Bn (2nd Pz Div): red winged serpent, edged white and surrounded by white diamond outline. White outline of shield was also used. Employed on Eastern front. **3** 6th Pz Regt (3rd Pz Div): painted on turrets in a number of different colours, possibly denoting coy within the regt; all edged white. **4** 6th Pz Regt (3rd Pz Div): yellow, used 1943-4. **5** 7th Pz Regt (10th Pz Div): in vehicle colour, with sprayed outline, white on dunkel grau, black on dunkel gelb or white. **6** 8th Pz Regt (15th Pz Div): red. **7** 18th Pz Regt (18th Pz Div): in 1941, as Operation Seelöwe was obviously not going to take place, those units trained in amphibious tanks were organised into 18th Pz Regt. This regt led the attack on the USSR by driving across the River Bug on June 22 1941. At this time the tanks had the sign illustrated painted in white on their turrets. **8** 21st Pz Regt (20th Pz Div): white. **9** 31st Pz Regt (5th Pz Div). **10** 130th (Lehr) Pz Regt, 2nd Bn Pz Div Lehr): two red lines on white. Painted on turret sides to commemorate cmdr, killed June 1944. Sometimes appears turned 90 degrees to form diamond, when it represents actual coat of arms of that cmdr. **11** 501st Heavy Tank Regt: black or white outline painted on front near hull machine-gun mounting and/or on turret rear. **12** 936th StuG-Bde (116th Pz Div): red greyhound's head on white shield edged red. Reconstruction. **13** Regt General Göring: in white on all vehicles of the regt in 1939-early 1941 period. **14** Regt

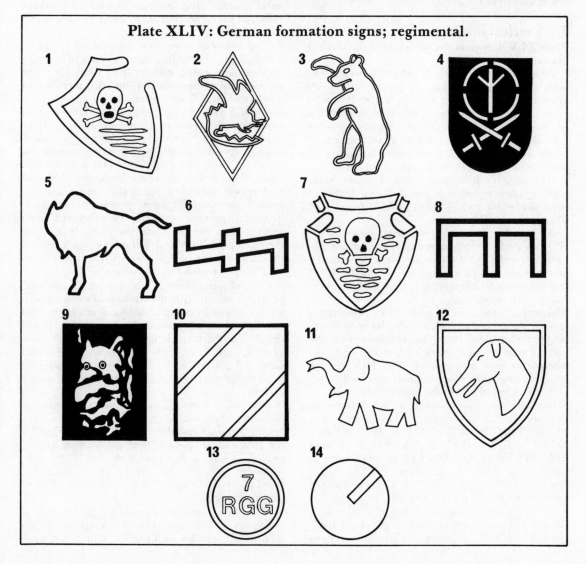

Plate XLIV: German formation signs; regimental.

General Göring: white disc representing clock face, with coy or btty number shown by position of indicator (2nd Coy is shown here). The indicator was green for all units except flak, which used red; 1941-late 1942 period.

6 Arm of service markings

Arm of service within the Armed Forces was indicated by the prefix to a vehicle's serial number (see section 10) and the branch of service within the Army by a symbol which formed part of the tactical markings, see section 7. In order not to confuse the reader unnecessarily, the complete system for tactical markings is described under section 7.

7 Tactical markings

Plate XLV illustrates the principle of the tactical marking system:

1st row: the basic symbols used to represent: a) tank units; b) Inf units; c) service units; d) armoured car units; e) signals units; f) motor cycle units. Below these symbols was added a second symbol to indicate type of mobility—*2nd row:* a) tracked; b) half-tracked; c) motorised; d) partly motorised. (Pz Gren units mounted in half-tracks sometimes used c instead of b.)

HQ vehicles had 'flags' added above their basic symbol to indicate the different levels of command—*3rd row:* a) Army; b) Corps; c) div; d) bde; e) regt; f) bn.

All vehicles in a unit, including those in the HQs, carried a branch of service symbol above the basic one—*4th and 5th rows:* a) Arty; b) recce; c and d) transport; e) signals; f) medical; g) maintenance; h) engineers; i) light engineers; j) radio; k) telephone; l) field post office. Maintenance and field post office sometimes carried their symbols within the basic symbol. HQ vehicles 'flew' their flag symbols from the vertical part of their branch of service symbol: where this was not possible the HQ symbol appeared above the basic symbol, and the branch of service symbol within the basic symbol.

Finally there was another set of symbols to indicate the basic weapon or equipment of a unit—*6th and 7th rows:* a) A/T to 1942; b) A/T 1943-5; c) flak to 1942; d) flak 1943-5; e) quad A/A 1943-5 only; f) HMG Coy to 1942 only; g) howitzer to 1942; h) howitzer 1943-5; i) Inf howitzer 1943-5; j) gun 1943-5; k) rocket/smoke launcher 1943-5, l) mortar 1943-5.

Several abbreviations and single letters were also used either within or to the right of the basic symbol: VERW. = Admin Coy; R = Regt Staff; St = Indep Bn Staff; le = light; S = heavy; B = Bridge Transport Column; M = Engineer Machine Platoon; W1 and W2 = Workshop Coys; K1-K11 = Supply Train assigned to a bn. Roman numerals (I-III) were used to indicate bn, or, in 1943-5 only, the vehicle mark. Arabic numerals (1-16) were used for Coy, Btty or Sqdn.

The examples illustrated in **Plate XLVI** should clarify any confusion over the appearance of the combined symbols. All these symbols were normally stencilled on front and rear of all types of AFVs and softskins, and were almost always in white, with yellow being used occasionally, although when necessary the symbols could be hand painted and on rare occasions different coloured paints were used to identify coys or bns within a div.

The symbols were first introduced in 1935, and brought up-to-date as new types of vehicles and weapons came into service. Later the signs were published in a booklet, and this was used as a reference by all formations when applying the symbols during the 1939-42 period. However, in January 1943 many changes and additions were made to the system and although many formations adopted the new symbols, others did not. The result was a mixture of the old and new signs, though so long as the basic symbols were understood within a particular formation this caused no identification problems. It does, however, prevent students of markings from setting down any hard and fast rules: it is hoped the examples illustrated will enable most tactical markings of this nature seen in war-time photographs to be translated by the reader.

Officially the basic symbols were 20 cm long by 10 cm deep, with the command or branch of service symbol on top standing 8 cm high, and the type of mobility symbol below being 1.5 cm deep. Numbers or letters added to the basic symbol were 8 cm high. In practice, size could vary, particularly if the signs were hand painted or suitable surfaces were limited, as on motor cycles.

One other form of tactical marking was the Arty bn or btty letter, applied to the sides of Arty towing vehicles and the guns themselves, and on the fronts of SP guns. These were single letters, only A-D having been seen in use. They were normally stencilled in white, but occasionally hand painted examples occur, and some of these employ black paint.

On a few notable occasions, special tactical markings were introduced temporarily to identify all vehicles within a formation, the most famous examples being the K for Pz Grp Kleist, and G for Pz Grp Guderian, implemented on September 10 and October 10 1940 respectively, for the invasion of the USSR. These letters were painted in white on the front and rear of vehicles.

The Hermann Göring Division, formed in late 1942, did not use the Wehrmacht system, but had its own distinctive system. Each vehicle carried a white disc painted on the front left, with a bar reaching from centre to edge, the two representing a clock face and hand, the position of the hand, or indicator, thus marking the number of bn, coy or btty. Staffs of regt, bn and coy had a small disc added to the axis of the indicator. Each type of unit had a distinctive colour for this indicator: Pz troops, black; Pz Gren, green; Arty including Flak, red; Recce, golden yellow; Pioniere, black; Signals, brown; all others a light mauve. Where two branches of service used the same colour, a ring was added to the centre of the disc, ie, the Flak Regt had a red indicator arm, the Arty Regt a red indicator arm with a red circle at the axis. Div HQ used a plain white disc: other admin units had various letters in light mauve instead of indicator arms: N = supply troops, V = admin troops, S = medical, Fg = military police, Fp = field post office, J = repair troops, except for Kfz-Werkstatt Kompanien, which had a K.

When the div was enlarged to a Fallschirm Pzkorps on October 1 1944, the same markings system was used, but new markings had to be invented for the new units: Fallschirm-Pz Gren Div 2 Hermann Göring used a white diamond instead of a white disc; Korpstruppen used a white disc on the diamond but with the exposed corners in red; and Corps staff used the same emblem with a golden Luftwaffe eagle above it.

Plate XLV (overleaf): German tactical markings.
See text.

Plate XLVI (page 95): German tactical markings; examples.
1st row: 1st Tank Bn HQ; Panther (Pz V) Tank Coy; Jagdpz IV or Hetzer Coy; StuG III Coy; StuG IV Coy. **2nd row:** armoured recce bn HQ; armoured supply coy; armoured workshop coy; armoured radio coy; armoured A/A platoon (sometimes shown over tracked symbol). **3rd row:** SP heavy howitzer btty; SP A/A btty (sometimes the calibre of the weapon followed the symbol); towed heavy howitzer btty; towed gun btty; towed A/T gun coy. **4th row:** truck coy

(120 tonnes capacity); rifle coy; armoured Inf, BN HQ; mortar platoon; armoured car recce coy.

Plate XLVII (page 95): Examples of tactical markings for Hermann Göring Division and Panzerkorps.
1 Div HQ. **2** 9th Pz Regt. **3** HQ 2nd Pz Regt. **4** 3rd Pioniere Bn. **5** HQ 3rd Flak Regt: red on white. **6** 6th Arty Regt: red on white. **7** Military Police: light mauve on white. **8** Corps Troops: white disc on red diamond.

8   Call signs
Before the war most AFVs within the Pz divs had carried a tactical number or call sign, which served to identify individual vehicles within a unit and assist the unit cmdr in directing them in action. Exceptions to this rule were armoured cars, which did not normally operate in formation and therefore did not need tactical numbers, and SP guns which in the early years of the war were, by and large, classed as Arty and bore btty letters instead.

The call signs were formed from three digits, and operated up to regt level. The first digit indicated the coy, the second the troop, and the third the position of the AFV within the troop. Vehicle numbers within the troops were 1, 2, 3 and 4, and troop cmdrs were therefore 11, 21, 31, 41, etc. With the coy number placed in front of these two digits you therefore arrived at, for example, 321, the first tank of the 2nd Troop (or 2nd Troop cmdr) in the third coy. Coys of the 1st Bn were numbered 1-4, those of the 2nd Bn 5-8, so a bn symbol or number was not necessary: tank 743, for example, would be the third tank of 4th Troop, 3rd Coy, 2nd Bn.

Coy HQ vehicles were identified by the numbers 01 (Coy cmdr) and 02 (CSM), with the coy number in front—101, 102, 201, 202, etc. At bn level the HQ vehicles were also numbered, 01 (cmdr), 02 (2I/C), 03 (Signals officer), 04 (Ordnance officer), and preceded by the bn number in Roman numerals—I01, I02, II01, II02 and so on. Sometimes the 01 might be omitted from the cmdr's vehicle, and only the bn number displayed. In some cases the bn cmdr's tank was numbered 00, the 2I/C's 01, etc, and the coy cmdrs' numbers were 100, 200, 300, etc.

Regimental HQ vehicles bore the same HQ numbers, extended to 08, but were preceded by the letter R—R01, R02, etc. There was also RA (Regt's Arzt) for the doctor's vehicle, and when Engineer tanks or ARVs were attached to

Plate XLV: German tactical markings.

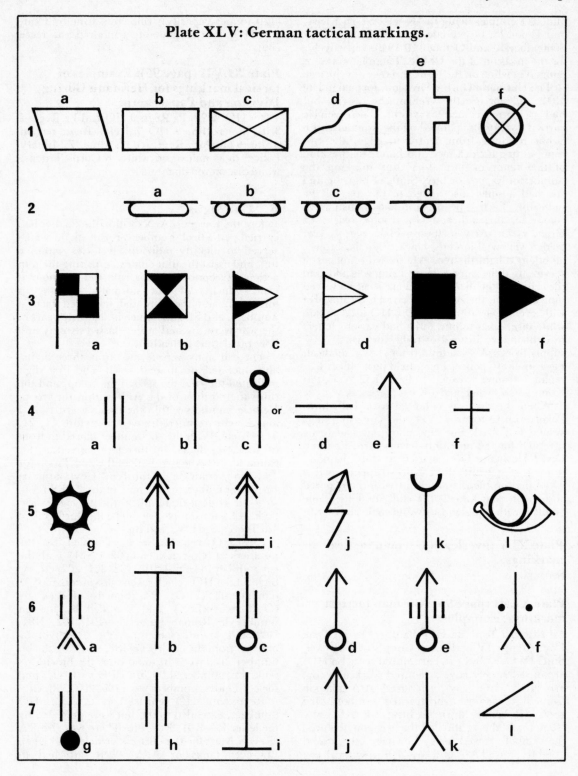

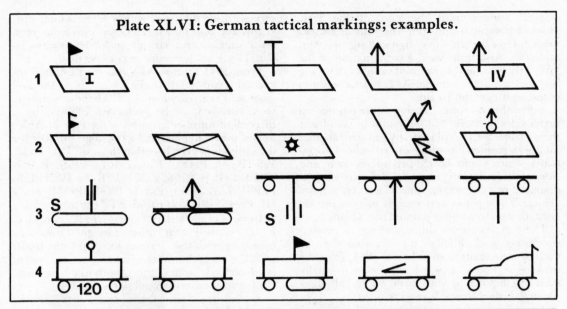

Plate XLVI: German tactical markings; examples.

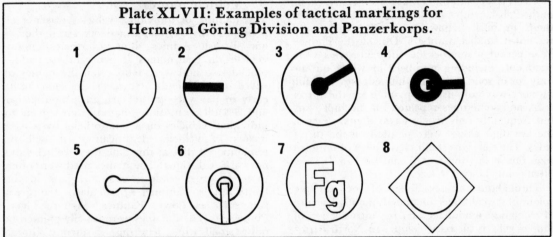

Plate XLVII: Examples of tactical markings for Hermann Göring Division and Panzerkorps.

RHQ they carried the letters Pi. Sometimes an HQ tank might bear a number followed by the letter B for Befehlswagen, or command tank, and in some regts the adjutant used the abbreviation Adj instead of his number.

During the course of the war, HQ vehicles came to be recognised as such by the enemy because of their call signs and a number of different call signs were used in an attempt to confuse the enemy. Some RHQ tanks carried 900, 901, etc, and others used 001, 002, etc. Other odd call signs were created by the appearance of 9th Coys in some divs (Tiger Coys) and in these units the RHQ tanks carried 1001, 1002, etc, as if belonging to a 10th Coy.

In April 1944 this system was standardised by the Inspector General of armoured troops. The new system, to come into effect by June 15 1944, was basically as before but now included the vehicles of SS and Pz-Gren divisions, and armoured recce bns. In some of these divs there were Inf coys equipped with Puma heavy armoured cars, and these became the 10th or even 11th armoured coys, creating call signs such as 1021, 1121, etc. In addition regt and bn code prefixes were abolished, and a two-digit code was to be chosen at random from numbers above 20. The Wehrmacht had other problems by June 1944, and these new codes were not universally adopted, many formations continuing to use the original system until the end of the war. However, some assault gun and tank destroyer units did not use the three-digit call sign system, and other Arty units used a combination of the bn or btty letter and a two-digit number denoting btty and gun, for example, A12, the second gun of the 1st Btty of the 1st Bn.

Before the war some call signs were painted on turret sides in white, but by the outbreak of war these had been replaced by much smaller numbers painted in white on rhomboid metal plates which could be clipped to the rear and sides of the hull, being removed if the vehicle was damaged or broke down, and placed on a spare vehicle. These plates were usually painted dunkel grau, though some units painted them black.

These plates proved difficult to see in combat conditions, and although they continued to be used by some units until as late as 1941, from the invasion of Poland onwards they were normally used in conjunction with large white call signs painted on the turret sides and rear.

These larger numbers proved too conspicuous in the Polish campaign and many units repainted them in dark yellow, or erased them and repainted smaller numbers. During the Phoney War period a number of different styles were tried out, including numbers in white outline only, or of solid red with white edging. The full number was now usually painted on the turret rear, and sometimes repeated on the hull rear, but frequently only the last two digits, or even the last digit alone, were painted on the turret sides. The call signs should have been of uniform size, but in fact the regt R and bn I or II were often painted larger in size.

Throughout the remainder of the war the colour of the call signs fluctuated, mainly because of changing camouflage and the introduction of dunkel gelb as the basic colour. In North Africa white outline or solid white figures were in use during 1941. This changed to red with a white outline in 1942, and later to solid black. On the Eastern front solid white figures were in common use in 1941, red and white in 1942, solid yellow or white in 1942-3, and red with white edging again in 1944 on Panthers and Tigers. Red numbers also appeared with a buff edging, but solid white or black figures, or just a white outline, continued to be used right up to the end of the war. When all vehicles were ordered to be painted in dunkel gelb, black figures tended to become more common on both fronts, and it was quite normal to see only a black outline.

Bruce Culver has suggested in his *Panzer Colours 2* that differently coloured call signs

served to identify coys within a bn: white, red, yellow and blue for 1st-4th Coys, with light green for a 5th Coy and dark green for HQ units. To date I have not been able to confirm this.

From 1941 Finnish AFVs on the Eastern front carried a two- or three-digit number on the hull front and rear in white. In 1944 these numbers were changed to the prefix Ps followed by a three-digit number identifying the type of AFV, followed by a hyphen and a two-digit number for the individual vehicle within the unit: Ps1- Ba32; Ps3- Ba20; Ps153- T50; Ps161- T26E; Ps163- T26B; Ps164- T26S; Ps221- PzKpfw IV; Ps455- ITPSV (AA tank); Ps511- BT42; Ps531- StuG III; Ps745- JSU152; Ps755- STZ tractor.

In view of the lack of evidence to the contrary, it is assumed that other foreign formations operating with the German forces on this front, with the exception of the Italians, whose system is described under the appropriate section, employed the German call sign system.

9 Vehicle names

The naming of individual vehicles was not as popular in the German armed forces as in the US and British Armies, but nevertheless many vehicles did bear names. In general these had no official role and were most often the names of wives or girlfriends. However, in some units early in the war—particularly in armoured car and assault gun units—names were given to individual vehicles on a semi-official basis as a means of vehicle identification: it will be remembered that at this date these vehicles did not carry call signs. The names used were often those of great leaders, cities, regions in the homeland, or animals—particularly the great cats such as Löwe, Panther, Jaguar, Tiger, Puma, etc. These names were usually painted in quite small white lettering, frequently Gothic script: on assault guns the name was often painted on the gun barrel close to the mantle, on armoured cars most often on the body sides.

One other form of name marking was the memorial to a dead crew member, a form of marking unique to the German tank forces. This most often took the form of a small rectangular panel painted in black on the side of the AFV's hull, with the crew member's name and date of death in small white lettering, or just the man's name in white directly on the vehicle. Only a few examples of these memorials have been seen, and all occur on the tanks during the first year or so of the war. They were probably only ever painted by the elite nucleus of the Pz forces, in memory of a comrade of pre-war days, and losses of such men and their tanks rendered the idea inoperable after the first great advances into the USSR.

10   Vehicle serial numbers

All wheeled and half-tracked vehicles used by the armed forces were required to carry a serial number: AFVs such as tanks and assault guns were exempt because they were not normally deployed on roads, as were some special purpose vehicles.

On most vehicles the numbers were painted in black on white metal plates with thin black borders. On the front of vehicles one such plate was carried, measuring 9 cm high by 47.5 cm long: **Plate XLVIII Fig 1**. On the rear of vehicles two plates were carried, fixed to the two rear mudguards. These were 20 cm deep by 32 cm wide: in the early war years the top corners were cut off, see **Fig 3**. On some vehicles, where it was not possible to fix a long plate in a central position, one or sometimes two 20 × 32 cm plates were fitted, or more usually painted direct, on to the front mudguard or mudguards. The construction of other vehicles with curved surfaces or smooth armour plating sometimes necessitated the painting of serial numbers directly on to the vehicle, and in some of these cases the black on white was abandoned and the number painted with stencils directly on to the vehicle in white. Motor cycles had a smaller curved plate fitted above the front mudguard, **Fig 2**, and the usual rectangular plate—though less than half the standard size—on the rear mudguard.

The serial numbers themselves consisted of a five- or six-digit number (extended to seven or even eight digits from 1944 onwards) preceded by a prefix to indicate arm of service: WH = Wehrmacht (Armed Forces) Heere (Army) = Army. WL = Wehrmacht Luftwaffe = Air Force, including flak bns. WM = Wehrmacht Kriegsmarine = Navy. POL = Polizei = Police, including all militarised police units. SS = Schutzstaffel, including Gestapo (in runic symbols). OT = Organisation Todt: changed to WT when the Todt Organisation became part of the Wehrmacht in late 1944.

Where civilian vehicles were pressed into service and were not given military number plates, the arm of service prefix was painted in white on a front mudguard.

A rubber stamp was also used to stamp an indelible dark red or black ink stamp on all plates, usually immediately after the prefix and often directly over the hyphen on the front plate. The stamp (**Plate XLVIII Fig 5**) contained each unit's Field Post number (down to bn and even independent coy level), which identified the unit for mail and official purposes. In addition, as a security measure, the serial number plate stamp could be compared with the stamp on the driver's papers to verify the authorised use of the vehicle.

For the tactical-cum-serial number carried on Finnish vehicles, see the end of section 8.

Plate XLVIII (below): German serial number plates.

See text.

11   Bridge classification numbers

So far as I am aware, no bridge classification system as such was used on vehicles of the German forces, but see rail loading classes in section 12.

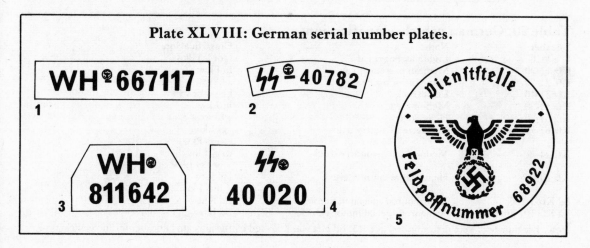

Plate XLVIII: German serial number plates.

1 — WH ⊛ 667117

2 — ᛋᛋ ⊛ 40782

3 — WH ⊛ 811642

4 — ᛋᛋ ⊛ 40 020

5 — Dienststelle · Feldpostnummer 68922

12   Shipping and rail loading marks

These marks were painted on panels on the cab doors of softskins and on the hull sides, near the front, or on turret bins, on AFVs. The size of the

Examples of loading panels.

1 On Tatra T57a light car (*indicates commercial chassis).

Kfz 1 Pkw	Kfz 1 (o)*
Leergew:	970 kg
Nutzlast:	420 kg
Verl Kl:	II

2 On Krupp-Schnauzer light A/A truck (* indicates cross-country).

Kfz 1 Lkw	Kfz 81 (gl)*
Leergew:	2600 kg
Nutzlast:	2000 kg
Verl Kl:	

3 On Mercedes-Benz 6 × 6 heavy cargo truck.

Kfz S Lkw	(LG4000)
Leergew:	5000 kg
Nutzlast:	5000 kg
Verl Kl:	

4 On Schwimmwagen.

Kfz	K2s
Leergew:	0.83t
Nutzlast:	0.45t
Ve KL:	II

5 On PzKpfw IV.

Kfz	Sd Kfz 161
bew	23t
Ver Kl	5

panels varied considerably, from large ones which covered most of a lorry's cab door to small ones of about 20 × 25 cm on AFVs. Often, owing to a change of camouflage, these panels became obliterated on AFVs, though some were then repainted. The panels were stencilled in white or black, many using screen-type stencils which produced clean, unbroken letters.

The information contained in these panels usually consisted of vehicle classification, weight when empty (Leergew), payload or load limit (Nutzlast), and load class (Verl Kl). **Table 20** sets out the Kfz (Kraftfahrzeug or motor vehicle) and Sd Kfz (Sonderkraftfahrzeug or special motor vehicle) numbers. The accompanying figures give some actual examples: it is regretted the load classes are not shown in examples 2 and 3.

On PzKpfw IVs and Panthers the size of the panel was often reduced, showing only the class number and weight class. Example 5 shows the panels painted on the sides of the turret bins of all the PzKpfw IVs of 7th Coy, 2nd Bn, 7 Pz Regt, 1st Pz Div, in Greece in 1943: class number, weight of the vehicle in metric tonnes, load class. No load marks have been seen for Tigers, but as these tanks required special transport, such panels were perhaps unnecessary.

13   Ambulance markings

To date no official regulations for ambulance markings have been found by the author, but from pictorial evidence it would appear that in general the markings as specified by the Geneva Convention were followed, ie, red crosses on white fields painted on the body sides, rear doors, and on the body roof. Those painted on the body sides were small, as were the two painted on the two rear doors, but the cross on

Table 20: German vehicle classifications.

Number	Name	Classification
Kfz 1-10	Light passenger car	l (or le) Pkw
Kfz 11-20	Medium passenger car	m Pkw
Kfz 21-30	Heavy passenger car	s Pkw
Kfz 31-40	Light truck	l Lkw or s Pkw
Kfz 41-50	Medium truck	m Lkw
Kfz 51-60	Heavy truck	s Lkw
Kfz 61-70	Light cross-country truck	l gl Lkw or s Pkw
Kfz 71-80	Medium cross-country truck	m gl Lkw or l gl Lkw
Kfz 81-90	Heavy cross-country truck	l gl Lkw or s Pkw
Sd Kfz 1-100	Unarmoured special motor vehicle	Sd Kfz
Sd Kfz 101 upwards	Armoured special motor vehicle	Sd Kfz

Note: Kfz numbers were discontinued in 1943. Sd Kfz was followed by the allocated number for the vehicle type.

the roof extended virtually all the way across the width of the body.

Although the ambulances were often in dunkel gelb or dunkel gelb and oliv grun, in the second half of the war, as the Allies gained air superiority, a greater effort was made to distinguish ambulances. Usually this consisted of painting the entire vehicle white, or the upper halves of the sides and all top surfaces, or just the bonnet top and body roof. Throughout the war Red Cross flags were also flown, either one or two, fixed by the cab doors or on the forward corners of the body.

Standard vehicles were also used on many occasions for transporting the slightly wounded. In these cases flags were flown, and small Red Cross emblems were painted on the doors and on the front mudguards and tilt sides on lorries. On half-tracks small Red Cross emblems were usually painted on the body sides and rear doors. On occasions only flags were flown on vehicles hurriedly pressed into service.

Some ambulances in north-west Europe in 1944-5 have been seen with a letter painted in white on a red rectangular background on cab doors: these probably indicate individual troops or coys within a unit.

14   Other markings

Chassis numbers: Many new vehicles had their chassis numbers painted on the superstructure in small black or white figures: on PzKpfw IIIs and IVs and Panthers these appeared just over the front machine-gun slit. The numbers were soon painted over on combat vehicles and were not renewed.

Convoy markings: White width markings were painted on softskins and half-tracks to assist visibility in night driving. In general these markings consisted of white edging on mudguards, the ends of bumpers, and on body corners. These white marks continued to be used, though to a lesser degree, when dunkel gelb replaced dunkel grau as the basic colour for all vehicles in 1943, but were not seen in the 1944-5 period. By this date red discs were being painted on the rears of vehicles, these discs bearing in white the distance in metres to be maintained between vehicles, for example $\frac{\text{Abstand}}{100\text{m}}$

Kill markings: These took two forms, rings painted round barrels of guns to indicate the number of Allied targets which had been destroyed, and silhouettes of aircraft, guns, tanks and even bunkers painted on gun shields. In the early war years these markings were in white on

the dunkel grau, but when dunkel gelb was introduced as the basic colour some kill markings were painted in red or black instead. The rings on gun barrels were most common on tanks, SP guns and A/T guns, and normally represented the number of tanks destroyed. On some flak guns a silhouette of an aircraft was painted immediately alongside the rearmost ring to indicate the kills were all aircraft. On gun shields the silhouettes were either quite large, with small bars to indicate the number of that type of target destroyed, or were much smaller, with one tank, gun, aircraft, etc, representing each individual target of that type destroyed.

Italy

1   National identification marks

No national identification marks seem to have been used prior to the armistice in September 1943, apart from rare examples of the national flag borne on a short stave and carried on the turrets of armoured cars in North Africa. The national flag was a rectangle divided vertically into three equal sections of green, white, red, and bearing on the white section a gold crown over a shield of the arms of Savoy; a white cross on a red field with a blue border.

Many Italian AFVs, especially the Semovente 75/18, carried German crosses, but this was mainly because the Germans themselves were using large numbers of Italian AFVs, particularly after the armistice. Lorries carrying Italian L6 Light tanks in the USSR have also been seen bearing German crosses, but whether these were Italian vehicles or ones supplied by the Wehrmacht is not known.

Tanks and armoured cars of the Repubblica Sociale Italiana (the Fascist northern Italy after September 1943) carried a small national flag, usually but not always with a yellow border, as a national identification mark. Units of CV and M tanks which fought on with the Germans (this happened in the Balkans, on the Eastern front, in France and Yugoslavia) had a wide vertical white bar painted on both sides of the vehicle to indicate their loyalty to the German forces: Light tanks in the Balkans in 1943 had a similar white band on the glacis plate and hull rear as well.

2   Aerial recognition symbols

In 1940 a white cross was introduced as an aerial recognition sign, painted on the upper part of the glacis plates of armoured cars, and on the turret top or engine decks of tanks. It has been suggested this was the early German Balkenkreuz, but it is more likely to have been the white cross of Savoy, which appeared on the flags of all Savoy regts. In February 1941 the cross was superseded by a large white spot. At first this was painted on the engine decks of tanks, but later it appeared more often on the turret top.

3 Rank, signal and other flags
No information.

4 Formation signs
In theory all the tanks and armoured cars within a div had a standardised div badge painted on the hull front, or less often on the hull sides. The size of this insignia was normally quite small. In practice only the Ariete and Centauro Divs can be proved to have done this, and neither used the standardised form of div badge on their vehicles. The shield insignia of the Centauro Div has also been seen on the cab doors of lorries in North Africa in 1942, suggesting the div's softskins also bore the insignia.

If a unit was not attached to a div, as was the case with most of the 'Cav' regts, then the regimental badge was used: see section 5. Some instances also occur of AFVs having the Tank Corps insignia painted on the hull front. Examples of all formation signs known to have been painted on vehicles are illustrated in **Plate XLIX**.

Plate XLIX (opposite): Italian formation signs.
1 Basic insignia for all divisions, the only variation being in name and number: 17 Pavia, 27 Brescia, 101 Trieste, 102 Trento, 133 Littorio, 185 Folgore, etc. Royal blue field, all else gold. **2** Centauro Div: royal blue over red field, yellow edging and centaur. **3** Centauro Div: black stencilled variant seen on 90/53 portees (Lancio 3RO) and Fiat-Spa-Breda 41s. **4** Ariete Div: royal blue over red field, yellow border and ram's head. **5** Ariete Div: black stencilled variant seen on sides of fighting compartments of M13/40 tanks, N Africa. Also used without shield outline, by 101st Bn, 131st Tank Regt, on turret sides of captured Renault R35s. **6** Tank Corps insignia, occasionally stencilled in black on hull fronts. **7** Tank Grp San Giusto (post armistice): national flag and tank silhouette, painted above machine-guns of CV33/35 Light tanks. **8** Tank Grp Leonessa (post armistice): M

for Mussolini, GNR for Guardia Nazionale Repubblica of the RSI or Repubblica Sociale Italiana. Also seen on side of StuG Ausf Gs' fighting compartment as a red M with yellow line through it, all on a grey diamond, in Rome, July 1943. **9** Todt Organisation: painted across hull front (to right of machine-guns) on CV33/35s assigned to the Organisation. **10** National Guard of RSI: yellow fasces, white flash, painted on both sides of turret on M15/42 tanks. **11** Camicie Nere (Blackshirt) Armoured Div: light blue diamond, red M, yellow fasces, painted on turret sides of German AFVs and some SPs used by this div from spring 1943 until disbandment July 25 1943. **12** Leoncello Grp, RSI: painted on sides of SP guns and tanks used by the group. **13** Lancieri di Novara: simplified version of regt badge, used on AFVs. **14** 741st Motor Section, 117th Motor Detail, 18th Motor Grp, 7th Motor Grouping of the Army in USSR: green tree painted on detachable circular white plate, attached to radiators of lorries of the section. **15** Unidentified unit: painted on cab doors of softskins of motor unit during retreat in USSR. **16** V Grp, Ariete Div: painted in black over yellow on sides of 75/18 SP guns used by group in N Africa. **17** Piscitelli's Grp: painted in red on sides of SP guns belonging to this group in Sicily. Names of ancient weapons were painted in white on the sign (for example, COLUBRINA and ARCHIBUGIO) and it is therefore possible this 'sign' was merely a background for the names, although all tanks seen had signs of identical shape and size. **18** PAI (Police of Italian Africa) fighting with the tank corps: light blue pennant, red crescent and palm, painted on both sides of AB41s used by the unit. **19** Bedogni's Grp: painted on gun shields of 90/53 SP guns of one btty in the group while in Sicily. **20** Bedogni's Grp: painted on gun shields of 90/53 SP guns of a second btty in the group in Sicily. **21** 101st Tank Bn (131st Tank Regt): seen on turret sides of captured Renault R35s. **22** 101st Tank Bn: blue over red, on turret sides of R35s, behind black horse sign. Blue and red are the colours of the collar patches for tank crews. **23** Unidentified unit: on wing of Lancia 3RO in USSR. **24** Unidentified unit: on front upper hull and turret rear of L6 tanks in Balkans 1942-3, red tongue, head probably light brown or dark yellow. **25** 67th Bersaglieri Bn: on hull front of L6 of bn in USSR; probably an isolated example, as appears to be cut out of metal sheet, either brass or painted white. **26** Leonessa Armoured Grp: on top left side of turret front of M13/42 tank of this group, Milan 1944.

Plate XLIX: Italian formation signs.

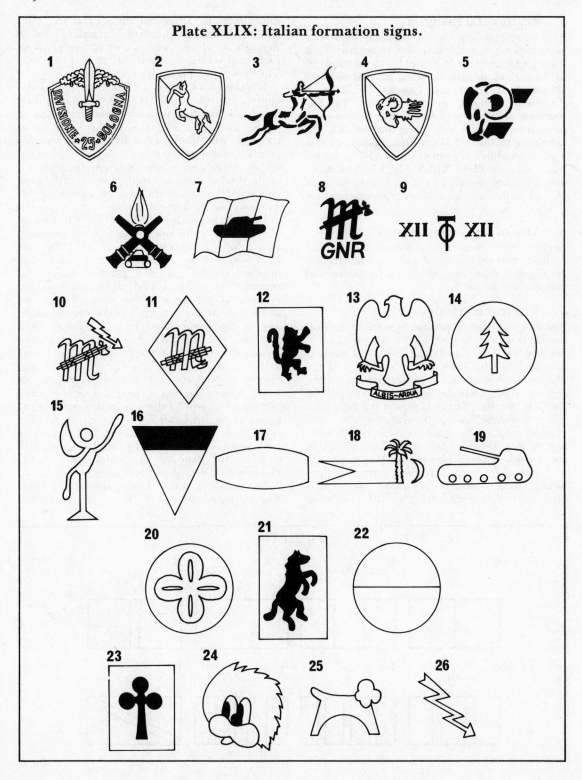

5   Regimental insignia

Regt headdress badges were officially employed as tactical signs in the Cav and some armoured Inf regts (see section 7), but only one example of such a regimental insignia being painted on tanks is known—that of the Lancieri di Novara Regiment, which served in the Littorio Armoured Div in North Africa. The insignia was painted on the right side of the hull on all tanks belonging to the 3rd Group (armoured) of this regt. A simplified version of the headdress badge was used, see **Plate XLIX Fig 13**. The same plate contains illustrations of all known insignia carried on the vehicles of other regts and various groups.

6   Arm of service markings

Army vehicles were distinguished only by the prefix to the vehicle serial number, see section 10. Cavalry regts were identified by regimental insignia, see section 5.

7   Tactical markings

Italian tanks had a precise system of tactical markings which was both simple and effective. It consisted of just a rectangle, with the various coys within a bn identified by colour, and the platoons within a coy by vertical stripes on the coy rectangle. Thus the rectangles were red for 1st Coy, sky blue for 2nd, yellow for 3rd, and, where applicable later in the war, green for 4th. Platoon stripes were white, one for 1st Platoon, two for 2nd, three for 3rd, and when applicable four for 4th. The marking for 5th Platoons was a diagonal white stripe, as five vertical stripes would have created a sign not easily distinguished at a distance. 5th Platoons were

uncommon in armoured units, and the only known example is the 67th (Armoured) Bn of Bersaglieri, which had two coys of five platoons each, and served in the USSR from July 1942. The bn was equipped with L6/40 tanks.

Coy HQ tanks used a plain rectangle of the appropriate colour. Bn HQ tanks were identified by a black rectangle with white platoon stripes as usual, and Regt HQ Coy tanks by a white rectangle with black stripes for the platoons. Bn cmdrs' tanks were identified by a rectangle in the colours of the coys within the bn, ie, the tank of a cmdr of a two-coy bn would have a red/sky blue rectangle, the tank of the cmdr of a three-coy bn a red/sky blue/yellow rectangle.

Until the beginning of 1941 all these rectangles were painted on the sides of the fighting compartments (on the access doors of M11/39s and M13/40s) and on the right rear of tanks. The number of the bn was painted above the rectangle in white Roman numerals, and the number of the tank within the platoon was painted in Arabic numerals below the rectangle and in the coy colour. From February 1941 location and numbering was changed, the rectangles now normally appearing on the turret sides and rear, with the tank's position within the platoon painted above the rectangle, and now in white. Some examples of the post-February 1941 system are shown in the accompanying illustrations: a) 1st Bn cmdr, two-coy bn; b) 2nd Bn cmdr, three-coy bn; c) coy cmdr; d) third tank of 1st Platoon; e) fourth tank of 2nd Platoon; f) first tank of 3rd Platoon; g) second tank of 4th Platoon; h) fifth tank of 5th Platoon.

Bn numbers were now painted in white Roman numerals above the rectangle on bn

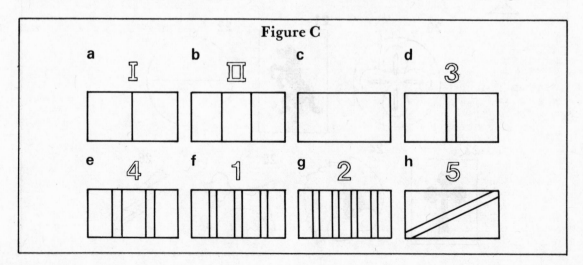

Figure C

cmdrs' tanks only. All other tanks normally carried the bn number in white Roman numerals on the right side of the hull, with the regimental number in white Arabic numerals on the left side of the hull, as illustrated by the accompanying figure, showing the location of tactical markings on the rear of an M13/40: on turret rear, the individual tank, platoon and coy markings; on left hull side, the regt's number; and on right hull side, the bn's number.

However, on rare occasions the bn number did still appear below the coy rectangle. AFVs in the USSR also carried the coy rectangle, with the tank number in the platoon above the rectangle in *black*, but on their hull front. The rectangle was repeated on the turret sides, with the tank number within the platoon normally painted forward of it, again in black.

AFVs assigned to independent Cav regts had an entirely different system of tactical markings in the early part of the war. The basics of this system were the regimental cap badge, regimental number, and the colours used on the uniform collar tabs. Thus the 1st, 2nd, 3rd and 4th Regts, originally dragoon regts, used a flaming grenade insignia with a straight flame, all in the regimental colour and with the regt's number in black on the grenade. The lancer regts, 5th-10th, had crossed lances in the regimental colour, with the regt's number in black on a disc where the lances crossed, again in the regt's colour. The Light Cav regts and Guides, 12th-19th, theoretically had a bugle horn in the regt's colour, but in practice at least some regts used a dark green bugle horn with the regt's number in dark green on a disc of the regimental colour within the loop of the horn.

Only sqdn and platoon cmdrs used this insignia, the sqdn leader's emblem bearing a royal crown above it, and the platoon cmdrs having above their emblems their platoon number in Arabic numerals in the regimental colour. Light Cav regts using a dark green bugle horn had the numerals in that colour, and the dragoon regts placed their platoon numbers *below* their insignia.

Other armoured units using the same system were the various armoured Bersaglieri bns, who used a bursting grenade and crossed rifles insignia, and some armoured Inf bns, who used their cap badge of crossed cannon, a grenade and a tank. For examples of this system see **Plate L**.

These emblems were normally painted on the hull sides, but the cap badge of the armoured Infantry bns appeared on hull fronts. Lorries and cars belonging to the Cavalry and other

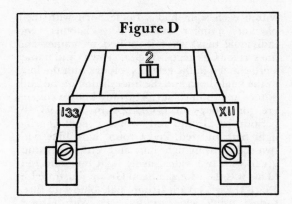

Figure D

armoured regts had their regimental emblem painted in black on the body rear.

The AFVs within a platoon were given the names of cities, battles, heroes, etc, and these were painted in the regimental colour on the hull sides and were underlined by one, two or three lines, normally in the same colour, to indicate the platoon number. Where a colour was common to two or more regts, an alternative colour was used for the underlining: this colour was the secondary colour from the regt's collar tabs.

Tanks in reserve had a large R painted in the regimental colour (or dark green for some Light Cav regts) on the hull side, followed by a number, 1, 2, 3, etc, for tank position within each platoon, and with the usual underlining to indicate platoon number. The colours used by the various regts were: 1st (Nizza) Drgns, crimson; 2nd (Piemonte Reale) Drgns, scarlet underlined black; 3rd (Savoia) Drgns, black underlined red; 4th (Genova) Drgns, yellow; 5th (Novara) Lancers, white; 6th (Aosta) Lancers, red; 9th (Firenze) Lancers, orange; 10th (Vittorio Emanuele II) Lancers, yellow underlined black; 12th (Saluzzo) Light Cav, black underlined yellow; 13th (Monferrato) Light Cav, crimson underlined black; 14th (Alessandria) Light Cav, orange underlined black; 16th (Lucca) Light Cav, light pink underlined black; 19th Guides Regt, light blue underlined white.

This unique system was abandoned as the war progressed—possibly early in 1941 when other changes to markings were made—and thereafter these regts utilised the tank marking system described at the beginning of this section.

Independent Tank Groups had a slightly different system to the above. The cmdr of each group had a bugle horn with the royal crown above it; the cmdr of each sqdn within the group had a bugle horn by itself; and the platoon cmdrs within each sqdn had a bugle horn with their platoon number above it. Platoons and individual tanks were identified by names and lines as for Cav regts. Bugles, crowns and names were painted in the group's colour, with the loop in the bugle horn and the underlining of the tank names in a sqdn colour. The only known colours are for groups of CV33/35s in the 1937-40 period: 1st Group: red with two sqdns, using light blue and red. 2nd Group: light blue with two sqdns, using light blue and red. 3rd Group: green with two sqdns, using light blue and red. (This was the Monzambano Group illustrated in **Plate L Fig 11**.) 4th Group: pale blue with three sqdns, using white, red, green. 5th Group: medium blue with three sqdns, using white, red, green.

Reserve tanks carried the usual R followed by a tank number in the group colour, with the underlining in the sqdn colour to indicate platoon. It is presumed this system was also abandoned in early 1941, and the marking system for armoured divs adopted instead.

The pre-war tactical marking system also seems to have survived and been used to a limited extent. It was certainly in use on Light tanks in the Middle East in 1939. **Plate LI (Figs 1-4)** illustrates this system briefly: 1) Coy cmdr. 2) 1st Platoon, cmdr, 1st, 2nd and 3rd tanks. 3) 2nd Platoon, cmdr, 1st, 2nd and 3rd tanks. 4) 3rd Platoon, cmdr, 1st, 2nd and 3rd tanks.

In this system coys were distinguished by colour: 1st, red; 2nd, white; 3rd, orange; 4th, light blue; 5th, green; 6th, black.

The 3-ton lorries of motorised Inf seen in a parade in Athens during April 1941, carried a unit identification in solid white on the bottom half of the body sides: $\dfrac{759}{\text{AUTOREPARTO}}$ (759th Motor Detachment). This is an example of the continued use of the pre-war system for marking softskins: it is not known if all softskins continued to use this old system, but it was certainly in use to a considerable extent in the early war years, in the Greek campaign, Yugoslavia, and in the USSR. This system was not used in North Africa, probably because all vehicles were repainted in sand camouflage when they arrived there. Under the system all vehicles carried, in white stencilled lettering on both sides of the body and on the tailboard, the name of the regt, the bn number in Roman numerals, and the coy number in Arabic numerals: see **Plate LI Fig 5** for an example, the side and rear of a Fiat 18BL (used for transporting Fiat 3000 tanks) bearing pre-war markings in white, and reading from left to right:

2nd Bn, first tank, 1st Platoon, 2nd Coy, Regt Carri Armati. Here the coy has to be indicated by a number because colours were not used on softskins.

Regimental names were often abbreviated, for example, Reggto Art instead of Reggimento Artiglieria. Motor sections attached to regts carried that regt's name, for example, Reggimento Savoia Cavallerio for lorries attached to that regt, and 41°Rgt Art Div Firenze for lorries of the 41st Field Arty Regt with the Inf Div Firenze.

Some Lancia 3RO lorries landed in Tunisia in 1942 were requisitioned civilian transport and still carried their private owners' 'markings'. These vehicles were used to shift military supplies from the docks to depots. Other civilian vehicles, belonging to companies working in Ethiopia, Libya and Somaliland, were commandeered and used by the Army, and these vehicles continued to bear their various company badges, etc.

Plate L (opposite): Italian tactical markings.

1 Flaming grenade used by Regts 1-4, here bearing 1st Regt's number. **2** 1st, 2nd and 3rd Platoon cmdrs' insignia for 1st Regt. **3** Crossed lances for Regts 5-10, here bearing 6th Regt's number and being the sqdn cmdr's insignia. **4** 1st, 2nd and 3rd Platoon cmdrs' insignia for 6th Regt. **5** Bugle horn used by Regts 12-19, here showing the sqdn cmdr's insignia for 14th Regt. **6** 1st, 2nd and 3rd Platoon cmdrs' insignia for 14th Regt. **7** Insignia used by some armoured Inf bns: note bn number in centre. **8** Bugle horn, crossed rifles, and grenade insignia of Bersaglieri bns. Bn number is carried on the roundel of the horn. **9** Variant of Bersaglieri insignia, stencilled on hull fronts of CV33 tanks of 2nd Bersaglieri in Albania 1939. **10** Tank name in 3rd Platoon (light blue letters underlined in white) of 19th Regt. **11** Insignia painted on vehicles of Monzambano Tank Grp, top to bottom: Grp cmdr, sqdn cmdr, 1st, 2nd and 3rd Platoon cmdrs, Reserve tanks of 2nd and 1st Platoons.

Plate LI (page 106): Italian tactical markings and serial number plates.

Figs 1-5 See text for explanation. **6** Number plate on left rear of Lancia 3RO ambulance, N Africa. **7** Number plate on glacis of M13/40, N Africa 1942. **8** Number plate on left and right sides of glacis of L6/40 in USSR.

Plate L: Italian tactical markings.

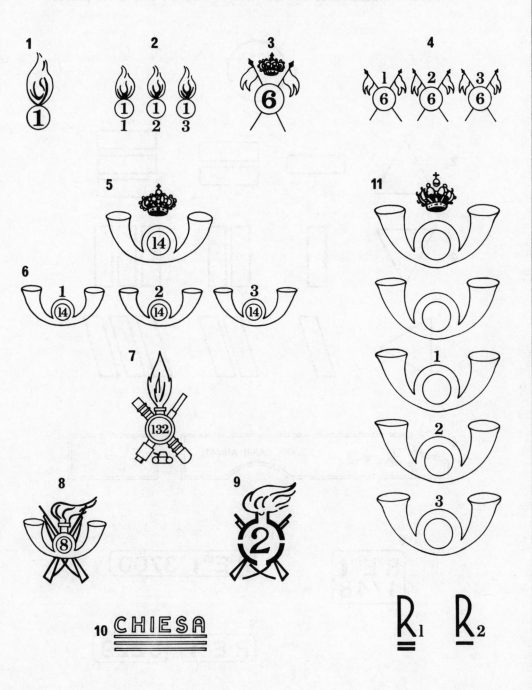

Plate LI: Italian tactical markings and serial number plates.

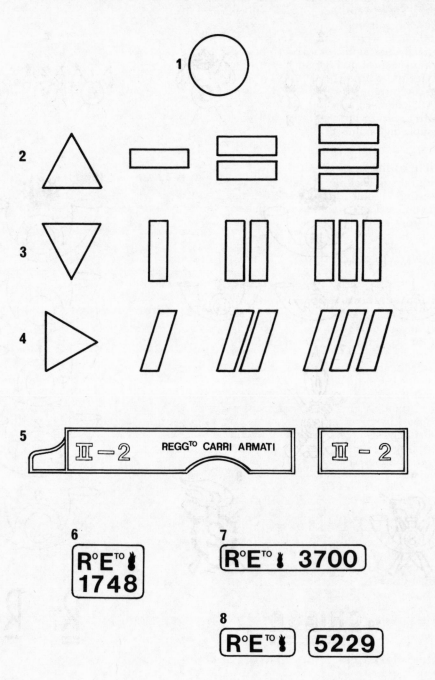

8   Call signs

Units of the RSI (Repubblica Sociale Italiana) used Arabic numerals painted in black on the turret sides of their AFVs as tactical signs after the armistice. These were single digit numbers, and were usually surrounded by a circle: both number and circle were stencilled and had the breaks normally encountered in stencilling. A similar form of tactical numbering, but without the circle, seems to have been used on some Light tanks and armoured cars in North Africa during 1941: examples seen are in thick black paint on turret rears or hull sides, and are either single or double digit numbers.

9   Vehicle names

In addition to the official names used as tactical signs (see section 7) some unofficial slogans were also used on tanks. These were normally painted on the hull front and might be either a motto, sometimes in Latin and occasionally the regt's own motto, or the name of a famous battle at which the regt had been present.

10   Vehicle serial numbers

All vehicles carried a white licence plate. Originally this was square and was carried on the left side of the rear only, but from early 1941 it was also carried on the vehicle front, normally in oblong form, though square plates were also used on the centre or left of the glacis on some tanks. All numbers were preceded by the abbreviation R^{O}E^{TO} in red, standing for Regio Esercito (Royal Army), followed by a red flaming grenade. The numbers themselves were in black and seem to have had four digits for all AFVs. It is difficult to define a precise numbering system from photographic evidence alone, but it would seem that numbers up to 1,000 were allocated to the pre-war Fiat 3000 tank; 2,000-3,000 to AB40 and AB41 armoured cars and L3 Light tanks; 3,000-6,000 to tanks and SP guns on the M40 chassis; with Light and Medium tanks also receiving numbers in the sequence as produced and not in large groupings by type. Softskins had four or five figure numbers, but their four figure numbers crop up in the 1,000 and 5,000 ranges, and it is not possible to arrive at any firm conclusions. For examples see **Plate LI Figs 6-8**.

11   Bridge classification numbers

No knowledge of any such system, but see the next section.

12   Shipping and rail loading marks

Lorries carried their net weight and load weight in solid white lettering on both sides, on the cab body just behind the doors:

TARA
Q 32
PORTATA
Q 25
} on 2½-ton Fiat cargo lorry

TARA
Q 35
PORTATA
Q 30
} on 3-ton Fiat cargo lorry

13   Ambulance markings

These seem to have followed the same pattern as the ambulances of other countries: a large red cross on the vehicle roof and rear doors, and a small white disc, about 9 in (22.8 cm) in diameter, bearing a red cross, on the body sides. A Lancia 3RO ambulance in North Africa carried a large *white* cross on sides and rear: if the vehicle had not been an ambulance these crosses could have been taken for the aerial recognition symbol. No other examples of white crosses on ambulances have been seen.

14   Other markings

No information.

Japan

Although many vehicles of the Japanese Army carried markings, there was no standardisation of markings as in other Armies, and all insignia painted on vehicles originated at a divisional or lower level. The markings did follow a number of recognisable systems but, being chosen by divisional or regimental cmdrs, were naturally of a temporary nature and were subject to alteration as cmdrs and theatre of service changed.

These vehicle markings were not recorded at the time in any official documents so far as the War History Office, National Defence Agency, is aware, nor has any post-war work on the subject been published in Japan. This means that all information has to be drawn exclusively from photographic sources and must therefore contain a certain amount of guesswork and almost certainly some misinterpretation. The problem is compounded by the fact that the censors obliterated from all photographs published in Japan during World War 2 any insignia painted on vehicles. Fortunately the War History Office has many uncensored photographs which do show vehicle markings. To these may be added photographs in the Imperial War Museum, London, the RAC Tank Museum, Bovington, and the US National Archives, as well as various newspaper and news agency files.

1 National identification marks

Two flags were used to indicate nationality, the national flag of the red sun-disc (the Hi-no-maru) on a white rectangle (**Plate LII Fig 1**), and the naval ensign of the sun-disc with red rays extending to the borders of a white rectangle (**Plate LII Fig 2**).

The national flag appears only on Army vehicles, painted in white and red. It is most often painted on the front right wing, or centrally or to the right hand side of tanks' lower glacis plate. Chi-Ha tanks of the 3rd to 6th Coys, 9th Tank Regt, serving on Saipan in 1944, carried two such flags, one each side of the lower glacis.

The red and white naval ensign was the recognised national identification symbol of the Marines, or Naval Landing Forces, and commonly appears on the turret sides of Marine tanks in the Pacific. However, the ensign was also used on the turrets of some Army tanks, for example, on Light tanks in Malaya in 1941-2; on

some Ha-Go tanks of the 9th Tank Regt on Saipan in 1944; and on the Chi-Ha tanks of the 10th Tank Regt on Luzon in 1945. The ensign was always shown with the hoist (that part of the flag next to the flag pole) nearest the front of the vehicle, and the fly towards the rear. On rare occasions an actual ensign was used, and this seems to have been a regular practice for Light tanks during the invasion of Malaya in late 1941. In these cases the stave was wedged into any convenient slot on turret or hull exterior.

Plate LII (below): Japanese national identification and arm of service markings.
See text.

2 Aerial recognition symbols

No information.

3 Rank, signal and other flags

Pennants indicating coy cmdr, support cmdr, and for each fighting tank, were used in China in 1939, but no details of the pennants are known at present.

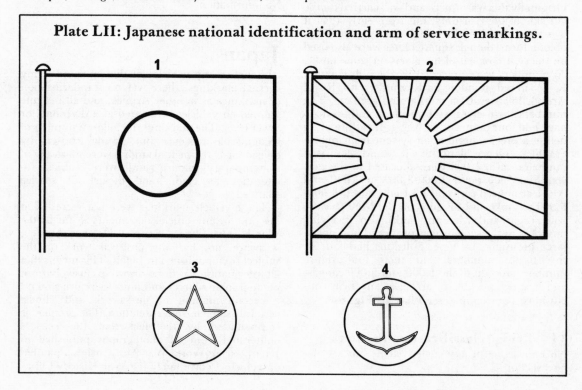

Plate LII: Japanese national identification and arm of service markings.

Signal flags were used in Light tanks during the early part of the war, possibly in other tanks as well. No details are known, nor is it known whether the flags continued to be used later in the war.

4 Formation signs
Not used.

5 Regimental insignia
Not applicable. A few regts used tactical signs which were painted on all tanks within a regt, but these were not regt insignia in the true sense.

6 Arm of service markings
The Army used a five-pointed star of the same shape as the Allied white star: **Plate LII Fig 3**. The larger tanks had a metal plate bearing an embossed star fastened to the centre of their glacis plates: sometimes the plate appears unpainted so that the star is of brass, but in other examples the star is over-painted. Some Light tanks had no such plate and the star was painted directly on to their glacis plates. Cars and lorries sometimes had a small round plate attached to the radiator, bearing either an embossed star in brass or a painted star on a dark background.

Early examples of the star are usually yellow (white on some softskins) but from 1943 onwards, as the Allied white star became more common, a red star with a narrow white edge was used. The stars were quite small, perhaps no more than 20 cm (maximum) from point to point.

Naval Landing Forces used an anchor as their arm of service symbol: **Plate LII Fig 4**. This appeared centrally on the glacis plates of tanks and was normally white. In 1944-5 the anchor was also used on the hull or turret sides in place of the naval ensign: see also under Tactical Markings.

7 Tactical markings
These fall into three main categories: single characters from the Kana or Kanji alphabets, and an occasional emblem from Mon (Japanese heraldry), which were painted on the turrets of all the tanks within a coy; geometric and similar designs painted on the turrets of all the tanks within a coy; and a few examples of bands painted round turrets to indicate either platoons within a coy or the tanks of coy cmdrs.

Almost 50 per cent of the examples seen have Kana or Kanji characters as coy insignia: they are listed in detail in **Plate LIII** and

accompanying caption. In all cases they were painted on turret sides in white: some idea of the differences in size is indicated by the drawings, the largest examples covering almost the entire height of a tank turret.

Practically all other examples of coy insignia studied fall into the geometric type: all the known examples are shown in **Plate LIV**. These were painted in white on turret sides unless otherwise indicated in the plate caption.

Finally there are a number of examples of bands of various colours painted round turrets. For example, one coy of the 14th Tank Regt, in action near Imphal in 1944, used a thin band painted around the turret just a few inches from the top, to identify all tanks within the coy. This band was probably red, and it is possible that other coys within the regt used bands of different colours. In the 6th Tank Regt, serving in Malaya in 1941-2, a similar thin band, about 10 cm wide, was painted round the bottom edge of the turrets on coy cmdrs' tanks: white for 2nd Coy cmdr, blue for 3rd, red for 4th. The 1st Coy cmdr's tank had no turret marking, and neither did the tanks in RHQ. At least one tank in the 9th Tank Regt, serving in the Marianas in 1944, had a broken white line painted round the turret several inches from the top: the significance of this broken band is not known.

Bands were also used, at least by the 23rd Tank Regt serving in China, to indicate platoons within a coy. In this regt each coy used its own insignia (see Kana and Kanji coy insignia in **Plate LIII**) *and* a number of thin white bands painted on the turret side: see **Figs 6** and **9** in **Plate LV**.

Plate LIII (overleaf): Japanese Kana, Kanji and Mon tactical markings.
1-4 1st, 2nd, 3rd and 4th Coy insignia, 1st Tank Regt, Burma 1941. Together these four characters form the word Tsukkushino, the name of the regiment's home base. **5** 3rd Coy, 1st Tank Regt, Manchuria 1943-4. **6** Coy of 1st Tank Regt, Japan 1945. **7** 3rd Coy, 7th Tank Regt, Philippines 1941-2 and Luzon 1944-5. Mon symbol. **8** Coy of 7th Tank Regt, Luzon 1945: see also **Plate LIV, Fig 5. 9** Probably 6th Coy, 9th Tank Regt, Marianas 1944. Mon symbol, possibly used as a regt insignia. **10** Coy of 11th Tank Regt, Luzon 1945. **11** 5th Coy, 13th Tank Regt. **12** Coy of 23rd Tank Regt, China. **13** and **14** Coys of 23rd Tank Regt, China. These two insignia were repeated twice on each side of the turrets, front and rear. **15** Training Coy, Army

Tank School, Japan. **16** Training Coy, Field Arty School, Japan. **17** Training Coy, Cav School, Japan. **18** Training Coy, Army Youth Tank School, Japan. **19** and **20** Unidentified coy insignia.

Plate LIV (opposite): Japanese geometric tactical markings.

1 4th Coy, 2nd Tank Regt, Guadalcanal 1942, on hull side, possibly in red. **2** Coy of 5th Tank Regt, Japan 1945. **3** Coy of 5th Tank Regt, Japan 1945, medium blue centre, white border. **4** Coy of 5th Tank Regt, Japan 1945, colour of disc unknown. **5** On tanks of 7th Tank Regt, Luzon 1945, on hull side just forward of emblem illustrated in **Fig 8 Plate LIII**. Possibly a regt sign, colour of central emblem unknown. **6** 4th Coy, 7th Tank Regt, Philippines 1941-2. **7**

Plate LIII: Japanese Kana, Kanji and Mon tactical markings.

Plate LIV: Japanese geometric tactical markings.

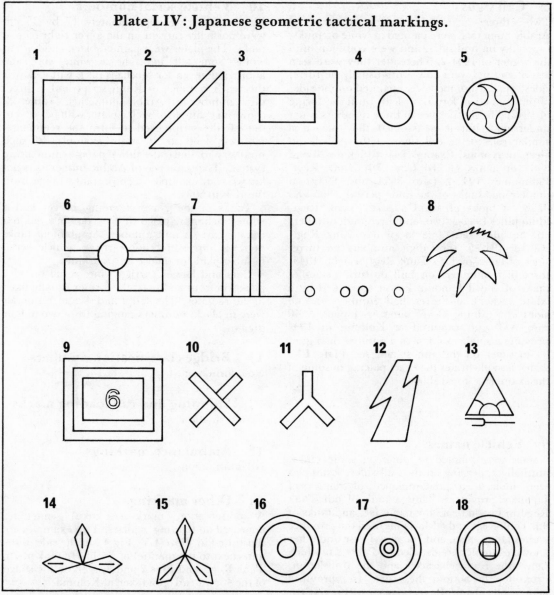

Possibly 2nd Coy, 9th Tank Regt, Marianas 1944, red rectangle with two white stripes, followed by red dots : .. : meaning unknown. **8** Unidentified unit, in white or possibly yellow on turret sides of Type 89B tanks, Malaya 1941. **9** Probably 6th Coy, 9th Tank Regt, Marianas 1944. Appears aft of Mon emblem illustrated in **Fig 9 Plate LIII**: white/red/white with small 6 in centre. **10** 14th Tank Regt, Malaya 1941, on left side of lower glacis. **11** 14th Tank Regt, Malaya 1941, on left side of lower glacis. **12** 17th Tank Regt, Japan 1945, white or possibly yellow. **13** Tanks of 34th Tank Regt, Manchuria 1945. **14** Div tank coy of 14th Inf Div, yellow, white or red on Peleliu 1944, white on Iwo Jima February 1945. **15** Unidentified unit, possibly a variant of previous example. **16** 18th Inf Regt Tank Coy, Tinian July 1944, and Attu May 1943, hull sides. **17** Unidentified unit, possibly a variant of previous example. **18** Unidentified unit, seen on Type 1 Ho-Ni SP gun, Mechanised Arty Regt, 1944, red/white/red on side of gun shield.

8 Call signs

Two-, three- or even four-digit numbers, in Arabic numerals, were painted in white on tanks, especially on hull sides, and were common until the winter of 1941-2. Thereafter they were seen less often, and were now more usually on turret sides. Similar numbers were painted on the sides of the bonnets of lorries, at least until the spring of 1942. The significance of these numbers is not understood, but it is assumed they played a similar role to the call signs of the Allied and German Armies. Examples seen include 20 and 8985 on tanks of 3rd Coy, 7th Tank Regt, Philippines 1941-2 (also 8924 and 8939 on unidentified tanks of the same period); 905 and 9758 on tanks of 4th Coy, 7th Tank Regt, Philippines 1941-2; two- and three-digit numbers on the hull sides of tanks of 8th Tank Regt, Rabaul 1942-5; three-digit numbers on turret sides of tanks of 11th Tank Regt, Luzon 1945; three-digit numbers on hull or turret sides of tanks of Naval Landing Forces (preceded by a white anchor); and three-digit numbers on hull sides of Training Coys' tanks in Japan. A 40 mm A/T gun captured at Kohima in 1944 provides a single example of a number on a gun: 94 in silver on the gun shield, see **Plate LV**, which also illustrates the exact placing of some of the examples quoted above.

9 Vehicle names

Names were painted in white on some tanks, normally appearing on the hull sides. Examples seen indicate a predominance of names of Japanese provinces. Thus a tank of 6th Tank Regt on Luzon bears the name Ise, and tanks of 9th Tank Regt in the Marianas used the province names Hi-go, Aso, and Nagato. These and other known examples are detailed in **Table 21**, which shows the Kana character and the translation. From top to bottom these are: Ise, province name, 6th Tank Regt, Luzon 1945. Hi-go, province name, 9th Tank Regt, Marianas 1944. Aso, province name, 9th Tank Regt, Marianas 1944. Nagato, province name, 9th Tank Regt, Marianas 1944. Script meaning Tokatsu, 9th Tank Regt, Marianas 1944. Script meaning Mitate, 9th Tank Regt (probably 6th Coy) Marianas 1944.

Abbreviations 'a' for cmdr's name, 'se' for tank (sensha) giving a-se, 8th Tank Regt, Rabaul 1942. Later in the war the cmdr was changed and the abbreviation became yo-se.

10 Vehicle serial numbers

Plates measuring approximately 17 by 35 cm were normally carried on the lower right rear of tanks. The plates were painted black and bore in white from left to right a white star, the abbreviation sen for sensha (tank), with below it the regt's number in Kanji script and a three-digit number in Arabic numerals. **Table 22** shows an example of such a plate, with below it to the left the script used to form the regimental numbers, and to the right examples of such numbers to illustrate the Japanese numbering system. The sequence of Arabic numerals is not known, but examples seen on tanks range from the 100s to 600s.

Tanks of the Naval Landing Forces had a white anchor in place of the star and did not usually carry a unit number. Amphibious tanks of these forces did not carry a vehicle serial number plate, or indeed any markings.

Cars and lorries carried white serial number plates on front and rear, the former usually fixed to the radiator. The script and Arabic numerals were in black, numbers ranging from two to four digits.

11 Bridge classification numbers

No information.

12 Shipping and rail loading marks

No information.

13 Ambulance markings

No information.

14 Other markings

A presentation mark (Ai-koku) sometimes appeared on fighting vehicles. Two examples are illustrated in **Plate LV, Fig 4**, on the side of the gun (next to the mantle) of a Chi-Ha tank of 7th Tank Regt; and **Figs 2** and **3**, seen on the shield of the 40mm A/T gun taken at Kohima.

Plate LV (page 114): Japanese markings.
1 Gun shield of A/T gun captured Kohima. 2 and 3 Enlargements of presentation symbols. 4 Presentation symbol from gun of Chi-Ha. 5 Chi-Ha of 5th Tank Regt, Japan 1945. 6 Tank of 23rd Tank Regt, showing stripes indicating platoon and central Kana character (i) for coy. 7 Marine identification emblem as used on tanks of 6th and 7th Naval Landing Forces 1944-5. Until

1943 these two forces, stationed on Tarawa and Makin, used the rising sun flag on turret sides. **8** 4th Coy, 7th Tank Regt, Philippines 1941-2. **9** 23rd Tank Regt, showing platoon stripes and coy symbol (each side of stripes—ko and wa). **10** Marine identification emblem, 6th and 7th Naval Landing Forces 1944-5: see different example in **Fig 7**. **11** Chi-Ha of 11th Tank Regt, Luzon 1945, Kanji character shi meaning warrior.

Table 21: Japanese vehicle names

i se		せ い
hi go		ご ひ
a so		そ あ
na ga to		と な
to ka tsu		が
mi ta te		つ と
a se		か み
yo se		て た
		せ ち
		あ
		せ よ

Table 22: Japanese serial number plates

★ 戦 一 **157**

1	一
2	二
3	三
4	四
5	五
6	六
7	七
8	八
9	九
10	十

34 三十四 3 tens and 4

23 二十三 2 tens and 3

17 十七 1 ten and 7

Plate LV: Japanese markings.

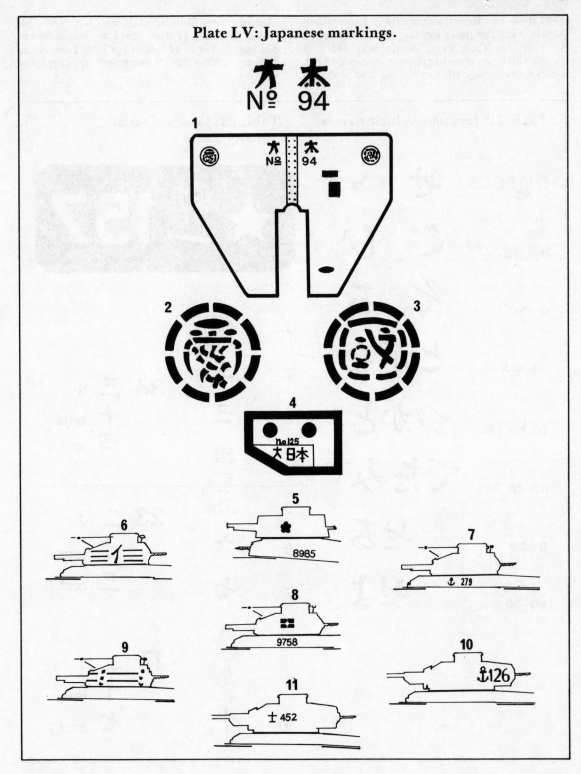

Sources

Anon *Carri Armati 2*. Edizioni Bizzarri, 1974.

Bender R.J. and Law R.D. *Uniforms, Organisation and History of the Afrika Korps*. Bender Publications, 1973.

Bender R.J. and Petersen G.A. *Hermann Göring: from Regiment to Fallschirmpanzerkorps*. Bender Publications, 1975.

Bender R.J. and Taylor H.P. *Uniforms, Organisation and History of the Waffen-SS*. Bender Publications, 1969.

Bingham J. *French Infantry Tanks, Parts 1 and 2*. Armour Profile, numbers 58 and 59.

Bradford G.R. *Armor, Camouflage and Markings, North Africa, 1940-43*. Arms & Armour Press, 1974.

British Army Council Instructions on vehicle markings, January 8 1941, February 11 1942, October 20 1943, with amendments.

British Ministry of Defence. *War Office letters (W032 11617) on formation signs and bridge classifications*.

Carell P. *Der Russlandkreig*. Ullstein.

Clark E. and Zadziuk S. *Char B1 bis*. In *Tankette* Vol 13 No 5. (Includes large section on 1939-40 markings).

Cole H. *Formation Badges of World War 2*. Arms & Armour Press, 1973.

Culver B. *Panzer Colours 2*. Arms & Armour Press, 1978.

Davies W.J.K. *Wehrmacht Camouflage and Markings 1939-45*. Almark, 1972.

Davis B.L. *Flags and Standards of the Third Reich*. Purnell, 1975.

Der Britische Kriegsheer, Wehrmacht handbook on British Army, published c 1942.

Feldgrau. German formation signs. Various issues 1954-6.

Formation Sign (journal of the Military Heraldry Society) for correction and additions to formation signs of all countries. Various issues, 1951 to date.

Fosten D.S.V. and Marrion R.J. *Waffen-SS, 1938-45*. Almark, 1971.

Futter G.W. *British Army Vehicle Colour Schemes and Markings of World War 2*. In *Military Modelling*, January-December 1974.

Hartmann T. *Wehrmacht Divisional Signs, 1938-45*. Almark, 1970.

Hider S. *French Tank Markings, 1939-40*. In *Tankette* Vol 9 No 2.

Hodges P. *British Military Markings, 1939-45*. Almark, 1971.

Kerrigan E.E. *American Badges and Insignia*. Leo Cooper, 1967.

Leslie P. *Vehicle Markings of the French Army in World War 2*. In *Tankette*, Vol 5 No 5.

Lucas J.S. *Command Flags and Pennants of the SS*. In *Modelworld*, June 1973.

Marec B. le. *Les Français Libres et leurs Emblemes*. Librairie Lavaizelle.

Milsom J. and Zaloga S. *Russian Tanks of World War 2*. Patrick Stephens, 1977.

National Geographic Magazine, June 1943: *Insignia of the U.S. Armed Forces*.

Odegard W. *Foreign Volunteers of Hitler's Germany*.

21st Army Group publication listing RASC company markings. 1944.

US Army Divisional Shoulder Patches. In *Philadelphia Enquirer*, August 1 1954.

US Army Information Digest. Distinctive Insignia (Cavalry), February 1964.

US Army AR850-5. Marking of Clothing, Equipment, Vehicles and Property. War Dept August 5 1942, with amendments of October 1942-March 1944.

US Army AR850-5. Markings on Motor Vehicles. July 1944, with amendments August 1944-January 1945.

US Army AR850-5. Markings on Motor Vehicles. February 15 1945.

Walker A.S. *Flags and Banners of the Third Reich*. Almark, 1973.

White B.T. *British Tank Markings and Names.* Arms & Armour Press, 1979.

Wise T. *American Military Camouflage and Markings, 1939-45.* Almark, 1973.

Wise T. *D-Day to Berlin, camouflage and markings 1944-45.* Arms & Armour Press, 1979.

Wise T. *Military Vehicle Markings I: Formation Signs.* Model & Allied Publications, 1971.

Wise T. *Military Vehicle Markings II: Tactical & National Identification Marks.* Model & Allied Publications, 1973.

Wise T. *Military Insignia.* In *Scale Models,* October 1969-December 1970.

Zaloga S. *Japanese Tank Markings.* In *Airfix Magazine,* March 1977.

Zaloga S. *Skoda LT.VZ.35* In *Modelworld,* December 1973.

Zaloga S. *Soviet Heavy Tanks of the Great Patriotic War.* In *Tankette,* Vol 9 No 6.

Zaloga S and Rosenlof K. *Finnish Armour 1939-45.* In *Airfix Magazine,* May 1976.

Many thousands of photographs have also been studied over the years, the main sources being: Photographic Libraries at the Imperial War Museum, London, US Army Archives, Keystone Press, RAC Tank Museum, Bovington; and the collections of photographs in such pictorial works as Purnell's eight-volume *History of the Second World War,* Odhams' six-volume *Pictorial History of the Second World War,* Amalgamated Press' ten-volume *The War Illustrated,* the Waverley Book Company's nine-volume *The Second Great War,* and the part-work *World War II* by Orbis Publishing Ltd.

Watch out for these other military books from PSL!

Encyclopaedia of the Modern British Army
by Terry Gander

Cameramen at War
by Ian Grant

A Wargamers' Guide to The Crusades
by Ian Heath

Hannibal's Campaigns
by Tony Bath

Alexander the Great's Campaigns
by Phil Barker

PSL Guide to Wargaming
compiled and edited
by Bruce Quarrie

World War 2 Photo Album Series
by Bruce Quarrie
No 1 Panzers in the Desert
No 3 Waffen-SS in Russia
No 5 Panzers in North-West Europe
No 7 German Paratroops in the Med
No 9 Panzers in Russia 1941-1943
No 12 Panzers in Russia 1943-1945
No 15 German Mountain Troops
No 19 Panzers in the Balkans and Italy

Tank and AFV Crew Uniforms since 1916
by Martin Windrow